1
IN THE MIDDLE

THOMAS J. BYE

Prentice Hall Regents
Englewood Cliffs, New Jersey

Bye, Tom.
    In the middle / Tom Bye.
        p.   cm.
    Includes an unnumbered introductory v. entitled Newcomer.
    ISBN 0-13-454398-X. -- ISBN 0-13-454224-X (bk. 1). -- ISBN
0-13-454265-7 (bk. 2). -- ISBN 0-13-454307-6 (bk. 3)
    1. English language--Textbooks for foreign speakers.   I. Title.
PE1128.B862   1995
428.2'4--dc20   95-5232
                                                                                                          CIP

• •

Publisher: *Tina B. Carver*
Manager of Development Services: *Louisa B. Hellegers*
Development Editors: *Tünde Dewey, Gino Mastascusa*
Editorial Assistant: *Satish Surapaneni*
Audio Development Editor: *D. Andrew Gitzy*

Director of Production and Manufacturing: *David Riccardi*
Editorial Production/Design Manager: *Aliza Greenblatt*
Production Editors and Compositors: *Christine McLaughlin Mann,*
                                                                Wanda España
Production Assistants: *Kelly Tavares, Bill Cochran*
Production Coordinators: *Dave Dickey, Ray Keating*

Art Director: *Paul Belfanti*
Page Design/Storyboards for Electronic
    Background Paintings: *Anna Veltfort*

Rendering of Electronic Background
    Paintings: *Rolando Corujo, Anna Veltfort*
Scanning and Electronic Art Production
    Manager: *Todd Ware*
Electronic Art Production Assistant:
    Don Kilcoyne
Realia Coordinator: *Wanda España*
Photographer: *Ken Karp Photography, Inc.*
Stylist: *Jozee Friedrich*
Additional Photography: *Steven Carr*
Photo Researcher: *Kathy Ringrose*
Cover Designers: *Paul Belfanti, Wanda España*
Design Concept: *Paula Maylahn*
Interior Design: *Curriculum Concepts, Inc.*

• •

© 1995 by PRENTICE HALL REGENTS
Prentice-Hall, Inc.
A Division of Simon & Schuster
Englewood Cliffs, New Jersey 07632

All rights reserved. No part of this book may be
reproduced, in any form or by any means,
without permission in writing from the publisher.

Printed in the United States of America

10   9   8   7   6   5   4   3   2   1

ISBN   0-13-454224-X (paper)
           0-13454380-7 (case)

Prentice-Hall International (UK) Limited, London
Prentice-Hall of Australia Pty. Limited, Sydney
Prentice-Hall Canada Inc., Toronto
Prentice-Hall Hispanoamericana, S.A., Mexico
Prentice-Hall of India Private Limited, New Delhi
Prentice-Hall of Japan, Inc., Tokyo
Simon & Schuster Asia Pte. Ltd., Singapore
Editora Prentice-Hall do Brasil, Ltda., Rio de Janeiro

INTRODUCTION

TO THE STUDENT

Welcome to **IN THE MIDDLE**. This book is written just for you! **IN THE MIDDLE** will help you learn English *naturally,* as you take part in activities that keep you talking . . . doing . . . and thinking — all while you are having fun.

You will meet new people and learn all about your school. You'll learn how to find your way around campus. You'll learn about the classes you need to take and about what it takes to be a good student. You'll learn about your school—getting a locker, following the rules, and ordering lunch in the school cafeteria. You'll learn what to do and who to see if you have a problem or need help.

You'll also learn new ideas and words that will help you in your other classes. You'll use new math skills to make a model of your classroom. You'll do an experiment and learn more about science. You'll learn about your neighborhood and the world around you. Best of all, you'll work with others. And . . . you'll learn English!

By the end of Level 1, you will understand and speak enough English to

- ▲ make new friends;
- ▲ tell about yourself;
- ▲ understand what your teachers want;
- ▲ tell others how you feel and what you think;
- ▲ take an active part in lessons in other classes;
- ▲ talk about the world around you;
- ▲ be a success in school.

You'll also begin to read and write in English. Your writer's **Portfolio** will give you a chance to share your thoughts and show what you know. You'll read poems that kids your age have written, and you'll connect their ideas to your own life.

This is going to be a great year! Have fun!

TO THE TEACHER

Welcome to **IN THE MIDDLE**, a comprehensive English language program that makes the classroom come alive. Responding to the unique developmental needs of young adolescents, every lesson promotes active learning and helps create an interactive classroom environment.

IN THE MIDDLE provides a student-centered perspective that reflects the personal and social concerns of today's adolescents. **IN THE MIDDLE** treats students as thinkers whose emerging ideas about the world are to be respected and valued. Students' knowledge, experiences, and interests help set the classroom agenda.

Lessons engage students in situations and experiences that stimulate discovery and discussion. Students have opportunities to express their own ideas and to hear and reflect on the ideas of others. Lessons provide students with opportunities to initiate their own learning. Open-ended activities give students the chance to think for themselves, make choices, and give input based on their lives and backgrounds.

The themes and topics of **IN THE MIDDLE** are aligned with current middle-level curriculum initiatives that promote understanding of the language in context. Task-based activities develop critical and creative thinking skills.

Students make connections of language and context across the curriculum. Lessons give students concepts, terminology, strategies, and skills they need for success in other classes. Students also learn how to learn. They reflect on their own habits of thinking and learning. They work at becoming strategic, independent learners.

Incorporating a communicative methodology, **IN THE MIDDLE** promotes acquisition through a content-based curriculum that is determined by the unique academic and social needs — and interests — of students in the middle grades. Materials develop both everyday language skills and the language proficiency needed for success in the classroom.

Themes and language forms are recycled; lessons make increasingly complex language demands of the student that are age- and stage-appropriate. Authentic language in context and lavish use of illustrations and realia provide students with comprehensible input.

Every unit integrates listening, speaking, reading, and writing and promotes interaction, thinking, and negotiation of meaning. Although grammar and vocabulary are introduced in context, language forms are not overtly practiced. Rather, grammatical structures, notions, functions, and vocabulary emerge naturally from the content focus of each lesson. Language use develops through meaning and understanding.

Finally students learn that working together works. A variety of activities involve students in learning cooperatively with partners and in groups. Projects and hands-on activities ensure high levels of interaction and create student motivation and feelings of success and competence.

IN THE MIDDLE is organized in four developmental levels.

▲ **THE NEWCOMER LEVEL** helps newly arrived students develop emergent and beginning reading and writing skills — and includes special support for the "silent-period" student.

▲ **LEVEL 1** enables students to move from the early-production stage to the extended-production stage of language development.

▲ **LEVEL 2** is designed for students who are beginning to communicate fluently and use language creatively.

▲ **LEVEL 3** prepares students for transition to the regular instructional program by engaging them in tasks that demand increasingly complex oral and written communication.

Let's take a closer look at Level 1. Level 1 takes students from early production to extended production. By the end of Level 1, students will be producing short utterances, and they will be able to function in familiar concrete social and classroom situations. Beginning reading and writing skills will emerge — often tied to personal experience and always within the context of authentic learning.

Organized around inquiries that relate to school survival, Level 1 helps students "learn the ropes" and introduces basic concepts and vocabulary across the curriculum. Level 1 methodology includes listening comprehension activities; naming, labeling, identifying, locating, matching, classifying, and sequencing activities; dialogs; open-ended production activities; questioning routines; and games. **IN THE MIDDLE** helps students become enthusiastic readers and effective writers. Students learn to read by reading. They learn to write by writing.

A writer's **Portfolio** extends the **Student Book**. The **Portfolio** helps students develop as writers, engaging them in a variety of activities that include expressive, descriptive, persuasive, informative, and real-world writing. Grammar and writing skills are embedded in writing activities that encourage students to write for different purposes and audiences. Each Level 1 unit in the **Portfolio** includes five activities.

An **Audio Program** develops listening comprehension skills. Students listen and respond to authentic conversations recorded by professional actors.

The **Teacher's Resource Manual** provides straightforward procedures for using each program component. Step-by-step instructions for the **Student Book** activities and language structure charts are provided. The **Teacher's Resource Manual** is designed to ensure that teachers new to the field will find everything they need to be successful in the classroom. Experienced teachers will discover a wealth of creative teaching ideas for enriching instruction and extending the material on the student pages.

The **Teacher's Resource Manual** also includes:

▲ A complete **tapescript** for the listening activities included in the Audio Program;

▲ **Reproducible Blackline Masters** such as a school enrollment form and a map of Kennedy Middle School, which enhance the hands-on approach to active participation in class.

▲ A **Family Links** section, which provides suggestions for strengthening the ties between the school and home. This section includes unit ideas for involving parents and family members in classroom activities.

▲ A **Literature Links** section, which suggests primary-language titles that teachers might wish to include in their classroom library, as well as titles in English that extend the content of each unit in the **Student Book** and are appropriate to the students' level of proficiency.

▲ A **Portfolio Assessment Program**, which enables teachers to evaluate each student's oral and written language development. All assessments elicit student-constructed responses and have an authentic focus. Because the assessment of reading and writing is embedded in the **Portfolio**, the teacher and student can monitor language development on an ongoing, systematic basis. Scoring rubrics allow the teacher to evaluate both the effectiveness and accuracy of student writing.

The **In the Middle Assessment System** consists of a placement instrument and end-of-level assessments. The placement instrument determines each student's initial level of proficiency in English. End-of-level assessments determine performance levels in oral and written language — allowing comparison over time and from student to student.

SCOPE AND

UNIT	THEMES AND INQUIRIES	EVERYDAY COMMUNICATION	LANGUAGE/ VOCABULARY IN CONTEXT
1 Welcome to Kennedy Middle School!	Institutions: Life at school ▲ How do I enroll? ▲ What classes will I take? ▲ How will I ever find my way around? ▲ What about the bell schedule? ▲ What can we do for fun?	Greeting people Giving personal information Identifying and naming people and places Telling time Expressing likes	Places at school Numbers Time Days of the week Sports Asking and answering *wh* questions
2 You'll Make a Lot of Friends!	Caring: Making new friends ▲ How can I make new friends? ▲ How do friends spend time together?	Introducing yourself and others Asking for and giving personal information Expressing likes and dislikes Talking about friends and classmates	Subject pronouns Present tense of *be* Contractions: *Both* Auxiliary: do/don't Affirmative/Negative: I like . . . / I don't like . . . Colloquial forms Object pronouns Sports/Activities Foods Asking and answering *yes/no* questions
3 I'm Taking ESL!	Institutions: Classroom procedures ▲ Where should I sit? ▲ How do I head my assignments? ▲ What are the rules? ▲ May I work with others?	Negotiating simple conversations Following and giving simple commands Following the teacher's instructions Expressing feelings Expressing likes and dislikes Suggesting	Location terminology: *at the back of, behind, between, in front of, near, next to* There is/There are . . . Singular and plural Classroom objects Subject/verb agreement
4 I Like My Morning Classes!	Institutions: "Learning the ropes" in each class ▲ What do we do in PE? ▲ What do we do in art? ▲ What are we studying in social studies?	Asking for and following directions Using a school map Expressing likes and dislikes Giving and following instructions Spelling aloud Ordering food in the cafeteria	Sports/sports uniforms and equipment Art supplies and materials Parts of the face and head Items in the cafeteria/ foods *Have* Singular and plural Possessive adjectives Simple past tense

SEQUENCE

LEARNING WITH OTHERS	CONTENT CONNECTIONS	READING AND WRITING
Sharing and comparing class schedules	School subjects After-school activities	Reading directions Labeling Reading a class schedule Completing a class schedule Writing a postcard Drawing and labeling a poster Locating and identifying places on a map Drawing and labeling a map Reading a bell schedule Reading a calendar of events Creating an activities calendar Filling in a form with personal information
Sharing a favorite book or other personal item Making a class yearbook	Understanding and demonstrating a procedure for making something	Labeling Reading directions Reading and writing simple sentences Making a chart Writing a conversation Making a Venn diagram that illustrates likes and dislikes (sports and activities) Sequencing items on a list Reading a yearbook Responding to a poem about being with other kids by drawing a picture
Working with classmates to choose a class mascot	Assigned seating Elements of assignment headings Classroom rules Forming small groups Steps in doing group work: brainstorming, discussing, and deciding	Labeling Reading directions Making a Venn diagram that illustrates *likes* and *dislikes* (foods) Writing a brief description Writing a classroom rule Reading and writing simple sentences
Inventing a new writing system that uses pictures Sharing posters and charts	PE: roll-call procedures Art: using art materials Social studies: interpreting a timeline that shows ancient civilizations; understanding a mini-lesson on the development of writing systems	Labeling Following written instructions Identifying and locating places on a school map Alphabetizing Understanding symbols vs. letters Completing sentences Creating a conversation Drawing a portrait Writing a description Making a personal timeline

UNIT	THEMES AND INQUIRIES	EVERYDAY COMMUNICATION	LANGUAGE/ VOCABULARY IN CONTEXT
5 I Like My Afternoon Classes, Too!	Institutions: "Learning the ropes" in each class ▲ Can math be fun? ▲ What are we studying in science?	Giving and following directions using a school map Understanding and following the rules of a game Adding and subtracting aloud Stating amounts in dollars and cents	Math terms Money terms Plants Animals School supplies Subject pronouns Simple present tense *wh-* questions: *what, who, when, how much*
6 Are You Ready to Work?	Institutions: Succeeding in class ▲ What does it mean to be "ready to work"? ▲ What if I'm late? ▲ How can I develop positive study habits?	Apologizing Giving excuses and stating reasons Following the teacher's instructions Explaining school work to others Describing a room Seeking and giving information	Simple present tense Subject/verb agreement *Why* questions Here is . . . Asking and answering *yes/no* questions
7 Let's Call Your Uncle!	Institutions: Communicating with home ▲ Who can help me with problems at school? ▲ What if I've been absent? ▲ Can I go on a field trip?	Talking about illnesses Using gestures and facial expressions Understanding and giving telephone numbers Explaining an absence Discussing common problems Offering suggestions Asking for and giving information	Body parts Simple past tense Destination: *to* Means: *by* (car) Places in the community Asking *where* questions
8 This is Our Student Handbook	Institutions: school rules and procedures ▲ What are the school rules? ▲ What about lockers? ▲ Do we have a dress code? ▲ Are there off-limit areas on campus? ▲ How should I behave on the bus?	Negotiating everyday situations at school Explaining a procedure Following and giving instructions Obligation and prohibition Giving advice Expressing opinions Expressing intention	*If* clauses Direction: *to the left, to the right* Numbers Items of clothing Location Commands Past tense Sequence words: *first, next, then, last*

LEARNING WITH OTHERS	CONTENT CONNECTIONS	READING AND WRITING
Making an "animal atlas"	Math games to reinforce computation skills Science: Classification of living things; characteristics of plants and animals A game of tic-tac-toe to elicit vocabulary of plants and animals Planning a simple budget for a class party	Labeling Reading directions Identifying and locating places on a school map Drawing and comparing maps Writing simple math equations Writing related sentences Developing a list Responding to a poem about doing math at the chalkboard by creating a new ending for the poem
Designing and awarding a certificate to the Student of the Week Comparing school logs	Organizing a notebook Preparing assignment sheets and homework schedules Offering hints Watching the time/punctuality	Reading directions Writing related sentences Reading common school forms (hall pass, assignment sheet, award certificate, etc.) Completing an assignment sheet Using cartoons to create a personal narrative Responding to a poem about homework by making a homework assignment schedule
Planning a field trip	School activities that involve communication with parents Reading a Fahrenheit thermometer	Reading directions Writing related sentences Writing a get-well card Reading an absence note Making a list Writing a simple narrative Completing charts Completing sentences Reading school forms and notices Making a billboard advertisement
Designing an incentives program for good behavior	The Student Handbook School rules Bus rules	Reading directions Writing words and sentences Reading lists of rules Prioritizing items on a list Arranging items chronologically Completing charts Labeling Making a poster Developing a money system for the classroom Responding to a poem about lockers by making a collage

UNIT	THEMES AND INQUIRIES	EVERYDAY COMMUNICATION	LANGUAGE/ VOCABULARY IN CONTEXT
9 Arms Straight Out!	Wellness: Physical fitness ▲ How physically fit am I? ▲ What kinds of sports and activities do I prefer? ▲ Why do we have to take showers in PE?	Giving and following instructions Expressing preferences Expressing likes and dislikes Giving reasons Discussing pros and cons	Direction Habitual actions: Simple present tense Ability: *can* Amount Duration Distance Sequence terminology: *first, next, then, last* Questions with *how many* Fitness activities Outdoor clothing
10 My Favorite Class Is Art!	Identify: Personal meaning in art and art heritage ▲ What can I see in a work of art? ▲ Who are some important artists? ▲ What appeals to me?	Expressing feelings and opinions Naming a painting Describing a painting Following instructions	Colors: Families and hues Lines: *Short, long, straight, curved, thick, thin, zigzag* Plane figures: *Square, rectangle, triangle, circle, oval, free form* Space figures: *Sphere, cube, pyramid, rectangular prism, cylinder, cone.* Art materials Questions with *do* Information question and clause patterns Count and noncount nouns
11 Let's Be Creative!	Identify: Personal meaning in art and art heritage ▲ How can I express myself in creative ways? ▲ How do cultures express themselves in art? ▲ Why do I prefer a particular work of art over another?	Expressing feelings and opinions Identifying similarities and differences Giving and following instructions Naming colors Identifying living things Describing paintings and other works of art Following a procedure Expressing preferences Comparing and contrasting	Descriptive words: *Long, short, curved, thin, thick, tiny, big, straight* Order of adjectives: *short, curved line; long, straight line* Result: *When you mix yellow and red, you get orange.* Repetition: *over and over* Words that describe texture: *smooth, rough*
12 Where in the World Is . . . ?	Interdependence: Living in the world ▲ Where do I live? ▲ How do maps work?	Expressing possibility Expressing certainty Locating and naming places on a map Asking questions Giving commands	Map terminology (political, landforms, and the globe) Location terms: *North, south, east, west* Division: *Divided into* Direction terms: *From top to bottom, from left to right* Questions with *where* Phrases used to express possibility: "It looks like a . . ." and "Maybe it's a . . ."

LEARNING WITH OTHERS	CONTENT CONNECTIONS	READING AND WRITING
Teaching others a new game or dance	Physical education: Exercise and fitness; team and individual sports; fitness tests; personal hygiene	Reading directions Labeling Writing simple sentences Prioritizing items on a list Interpreting and creating a bar graph Completing charts Writing simple explanations Reading measurements using a tape measure Drawing and labeling a picture Responding to a poem about playing sports by drawing a picture
Making a group collage Sharing favorite paintings and colors Comparing paintings	Visual art: Elements of design (color, line, shape); responding to art; art heritage; creative expression; concept of abstract art	Reading directions Developing a list Writing related sentences Completing charts Completing a paragraph Drawing a portrait Labeling objects Writing a description Making a collage with letters Following written instructions
Sharing and describing decorative artwork or objects from various cultures Describing living things	Visual art: Principles of design (texture, pattern); responding to art; creative expression; art heritage; evaluating art Doing research on an artist	Reading directions Writing a description Completing charts Writing a paragraph Writing a short evaluation Labeling illustrations Identifying patterns in a poem about cafeteria food
Making classroom, school, and neighborhood maps Estimating and measuring distances Playing bingo to elicit geographical information Making a class "quilt" about a community	Social studies: Kinds of maps (neighborhood and city; political and physical; world map) Concepts and terms related to geography and maps: symbols and keys; scale; grids; landforms and bodies of water; how the globe is divided	Labeling Reading and designing various kinds of maps Consulting atlases, encyclopedias, geography texts, etc. Using context to determine the meaning of unknown words in the poem, "Door Number Four"

UNIT	THEMES AND INQUIRIES	EVERYDAY COMMUNICATION	LANGUAGE/ VOCABULARY IN CONTEXT
13 Let's Find Out!	Identity: Thinking and working like a scientist ▲ What do scientists do? ▲ How do scientists make new discoveries?	Guessing Naming materials needed for an experiment Describing how things taste, look, feel, and smell Expressing preferences	Stative verbs: *taste, look, feel, smell, see* Descriptive adjectives Foods and spices Comparisons: *Whiter, whitest, least white* Change verbs: *turns hard, gets thick, dissolves* Cause and effect Prediction: *will* Sound words: *buzz, hum, ring*, etc.
14 Let's Celebrate!	Identity: Holidays, traditions, and symbols ▲ What are our national holidays and what do they mean? ▲ Who are some important people in American history? ▲ What are some important American symbols and traditions?	Discussing holidays Talking about past historical events Performing a scene from a play Describing the four seasons Reciting the "Pledge of Allegiance"	Months and dates Historical present Information question patterns: *What, when, how many* Intention: *Will*
15 What's Math Good for, Anyway?	Identity: Thinking and working like a mathematician ▲ How can I use math in my life?	Expressing possibility Expressing certainty Describing the dimensions of objects Following step-by-step instructions	Measurement terminology: length/width/height Questions with *How long, wide, high*, and *how many* Negative auxiliary: *don't*
16 What a Great School Year!	Identity: Reflecting on personal abilities and accomplishments ▲ What have I learned this year? ▲ What work am I most proud of? ▲ How good is my English?	Understanding an explanation Describing people Playing a guessing game Performing a short skit Interviewing Asking and answering questions Recounting a personal experience	Ability Frequency Simple past tense Temporary events: *-ing*

LEARNING WITH OTHERS	CONTENT CONNECTIONS	READING AND WRITING
Doing a scientific experiment Sharing collages Brainstorming	Science: Setting up for an experiment; equipment and materials; steps in the scientific method; safety procedures; tools of a scientist.	Completing charts Writing related sentences Labeling Understanding safety rules Writing a paragraph
Making an international calendar of holidays from around the world Making colonial ink and pen Writing a "declaration" using the colonial style of writing Drawing pictures of families celebrating important holidays	U.S. history: Holidays, important historical events, George Washington and Abraham Lincoln, patriotic words and symbols Holidays from around the world "America, the Beautiful" "Pledge of Allegiance"	Reading a calendar Reading dialogs from a play Reading a timeline Completing charts Reading maps Writing a short description Writing short paragraphs Designing posters Developing a list Responding to the poem, "Martin Luther King," by drawing and writing about a hero
Making a model of a classroom to scale Sharing models	Mathematics: proportion and measurement (figuring area and volume); estimating and verifying Standard and metric measurement Occupations that use math	Completing charts Labeling Writing brief descriptions Writing a comparison Making a floor plan Responding to Sandburg's poem "Arithmetic" by writing a list poem
Reflecting with others on language development Sharing drawings or pictures of favorite activities Summarizing the year through a game of tic-tac-toe Solving a problem	Metalinguistic awareness: Reflecting on one's proficiency in a language Portfolios: Assembling one's best work Understanding that one acquires language through ideas and through learning about the world	Completing charts Making a mind map Completing a survey Making a poster Developing a list Writing postcards Writing a letter Responding to a poem about teachers and grades by relating a personal experience

ACKNOWLEDGMENTS

The author would like to thank and acknowledge the following people, whose insights, suggestions and hard work helped shape this project:

David Bohne for his encouragement, enthusiasm, and support; the staff of the San Leandro (California) Community Library for research assistance; Tina Carver for promoting and celebrating the project from beginning to end; Tünde Dewey, Louisa Hellegers, Gino Mastascusa, Tom Dare, Johanna Evans, and all the other folks on the PHR team; Roger Olsen for his help in launching the project and providing feedback in its initial stages; teachers of the Vallejo City Unified School District, whose ideas are reflected in various activities (especially Unit 13, derived from science-based ESL curriculum developed by Bonnie August); and, finally, Steve Krashen, whose extraordinary thinking provides the inspiration for this project.

ILLUSTRATIONS

Storyboards for electronic background paintings: Anna Veltfort

Rendering of electronic background paintings: Rolando Corujo, Anna Veltfort

Dartmouth Publishing, Inc.: pages 5, 36, 55 (top), 72, 100, 102, 103, 116, 117, 124 (bottom middle)

DM Graphics: pages 111 (bottom), 112 (bottom left)

Michelle Desveaux: pages 78, 80

North Market Street Graphics, Mark Ammerman, Art Director: pages 6, 8, 10, 15, 19, 26, 28, 29, 30, 31, 32, 33, 37, 38, 39, 40, 45, 50, 54, 55, 62, 67, 70, 72, 74, 75, 77, 79, 82, 83, 84, 95, 104, 112 (top right), 114 (top middle), 124 (bottom right)

Siren Design: page 7

Taurins Design Associates: pages 11, 13, 27, 51, 53, 55 (bottom left), 59, 63, 68, 80, 87, 88, 98, 115, 118, 119, 120, 124 (top right), 128

Denise Whitaker's 7th grade class, George Washington Middle School, Ridgewood, N.J.: Ella Biggadike, Kim Brettschneider, Lauren Connolly, Matt Geyer, Michelle Hodgetts, Andrew Lane, Gabrielle Latourette, Janis Nava, Brian Nazzaro, Brenna Cheslack-Postava, Jessica Rhoten, Meredith Ruggles, Luren Shurtleff, Katie Latanich, Lauren Varallo, Morgan Wiss: pages 81, 84, 86, 87, 88, 109

Handwriting samples provided by George Polasky's 7th grade students, Our Lady of Czestochowa, Jersey City, N.J.: Oktawia Wojcik and Sadia Ali

REALIA

Paul Belfanti: pages 8, 20, 21, 39, 42, 48 (top), 54, 63, 66, 67, 68, 69, 102, 103, 104, 106, 107, 114, 123, 127

Wanda España: pages 22, 56

Ken Liao: pages 60, 71, 78, 89, 90 (top), 109, 125 (125)

Lido Graphics: pages 2, 6, 12, 14, 43 (left), 45, 46, 47, 55, 58, 62 (middle bottom), 64, 85, 86, 90 (bottom), 99, 101, 122, 126 (top)

Siren Design: pages 4, 16, 25, 33, 34, 35, 36, 62 (top), 91, 92, 93, 94, 96, 108, 112 (bottom right)

Paula Williams: pages 43 (right), 44, 48 (bottom), 52, 72, 75, 83, 115, 123, 124, 125 (left), 126 (bottom)

PHOTOS

Photographer: Ken Karp Photography, Inc.

Pages 73 and 76 by Vincent van Gogh, "Starry Night," 1853-1890. Dutch Museum of Modern Art, New York by Superstock; page 76 by Piet Mondrian, "Broadway Boogie Woogie," 1872-1944. Dutch. Museum of Modern Art, New York; page 85 (top left, bottom left, bottom right) by The Granger Collection; page 85 (top right) by Canadian Museum of Civilization; page 110 (top) "Washington Crossing the Delaware," by Art Resource/Johnson Eastman/Private collection; page 110 (bottom left, bottom right) by The Granger Collection; page 111 (top left, bottom left) by The Granger Collection; page 111 (middle) by Superstock

PERMISSIONS

Pages 34 and 35: Target Addition and Value of Words, respectively. ©1986 Regents, University of California at Berkeley. Reprinted from *FAMILY MATH*, Lawrence Hall of Science, Berkeley, California 94720; page 56: school notices. Used by permission of Essential Productions, P.O. Box 361, San Ramon, CA 94583; page 95: U.S. physical map. ©1995 Silver Burdett Ginn Inc. Used by permission of Silver Burdett Ginn Inc. All rights reserved; page 97: Adaptation from *Teacher's Guide for Mystery Powders: Properties of White Powders* by Del Alberti, Robert J. Davitt, Thomas A. Ferguson, and Susan Oakey Repass ©1974. Used by permission of the publisher, McGraw-Hill, Inc., 1221 Avenue of the Americas, New York, NY 10020.

REVIEWERS AND CONSULTANTS

Prentice Hall Regents would like to thank the following reviewers of **IN THE MIDDLE**, whose comments and suggestions have helped to shape the content and format of the series: Rick Amstutz, ESL Teacher, Pinellas County, Florida; Susan Dunlap, Program Assistant, Bilingual/ELD Staff Development, West Contra Costa, California; Rosalinda Feliciano, ESL Teacher, Dade County, Florida; Reisa Freehling, ESL Coordinator, Bainbridge Island, Washington; Paige Oliver, Crystal Beach, Florida; Ray Ramirez, ESL Teacher/State Trainer, St. Lucie, Florida; Debra Schwabbe, ESL Teacher, Franklin J.H.S., Hillsborough County, Tampa, Florida; Elizabeth Shurak, Multicultural Department Head/ESL Teacher, Broward County, Florida; Steve Sloan, ESL Coordinator, James Monroe H.S., North Hills, California.

UNIT 1
WELCOME TO KENNEDY MIDDLE SCHOOL!

TUNING IN. Look at the picture. Listen to the conversation.

Now listen one more time. Point to the person who is speaking.

Mrs. Smith:	Hello. May I help you?
Uncle Carlos:	Yes. I'd like to enroll my nephew. His name is Juan Ortíz.
Mrs. Smith:	Juan, please fill out our enrollment form.
Juan:	OK.
Mrs. Smith:	How old are you, Juan?
Uncle Carlos:	He's thirteen. He doesn't speak much English.
Mrs. Smith:	He'll need to see Ms. Vasquez. She's our sixth-grade counselor.
Uncle Carlos:	Thank you very much.
Mrs. Smith:	Welcome to Kennedy Middle School, Juan!
Juan:	Thank you.

LISTENING IN. What does Ms. Vasquez give Juan?

READING ALOUD.

Read Juan's class schedule.

TALKING IT OVER.

Name Juan's teachers.

1. Name Juan's science teacher.
2. Name Juan's art teacher.
3. Name Juan's PE teacher.
4. Name Juan's ESL teacher.
5. Name Juan's social studies teacher.
6. Name Juan's math teacher.

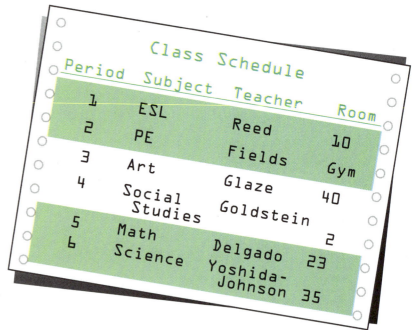

WRITING AND SHARING. What is your class schedule? Who are your teachers? Make a chart. Fill in your schedule. Then share it with a partner.

FIGURING IT OUT. Look at the picture. Name each teacher.

TUNING IN.

Look at the picture of Juan's teachers again. Listen as each teacher tells what subject he or she teaches. Point to the teacher who is speaking.

TALKING IT OVER.

Ask and answer with your classmates.

1. What does Mr. Glaze teach?
2. What does Ms. Yoshida-Johnson teach?
3. What does Ms. Reed teach?
4. What does Mr. Fields teach?
5. What does Ms. Goldstein teach?

 Make a poster about your teachers. Use words and pictures to tell what each person teaches.

Unit 1 3

LISTENING IN.

Who is Juan's buddy?

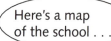

Here's a map of the school . . .

Ms. Vasquez: I'd like you to meet Chip Kowalski. He's your "buddy." Every new student has a buddy.
Chip: How's it going?
Ms. Vasquez: Juan speaks Spanish. He's from Mexico.
Chip: Oh! . . . ¡Hola! ¿Qué tal?
Ms. Vasquez: Chip is taking Spanish.
Juan: ¡Bien, gracias! ¿Y tú?

READING ALOUD. Name the places on the school map.

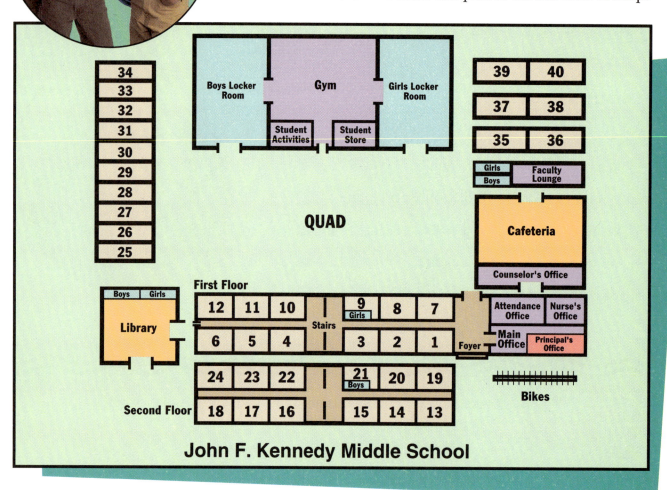

John F. Kennedy Middle School

4   Unit 1

FIGURING IT OUT. Find important places at Kennedy Middle School.

1. Point to the main office.
2. Point to the library.
3. Point to the gym.
4. Point to the cafeteria.
5. Point to the counselor's office.
6. Point to the girls bathroom.
7. Point to the boys locker room.
8. Point to the science lab.

a.

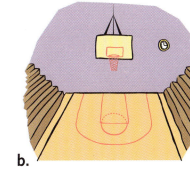
b.

c.

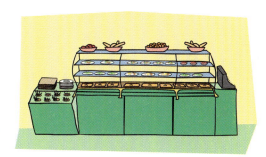
d.

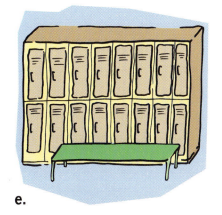
e.

f.

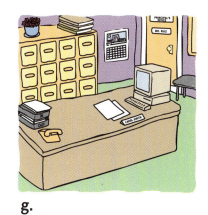
g.

h.

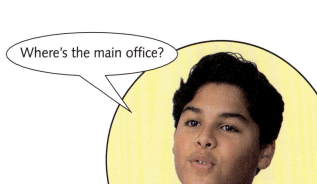

Where's the main office?

TUNING IN. Look at the school map again. Listen to the students' questions. Point to each place that the students ask about.

LISTENING IN.

What is Chip showing Juan?

"Here is our bell schedule! Period 1 begins at 8:15 and ends at 9:10. Period 2 begins at 9:15 and ends at 10:10 . . ."

READING ALOUD.

Read Kennedy's bell schedule.

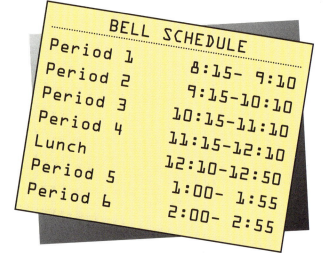

BELL SCHEDULE
Period 1   8:15 – 9:10
Period 2   9:15 – 10:10
Period 3   10:15 – 11:10
Period 4   11:15 – 12:10
Lunch   12:10 – 12:50
Period 5   1:00 – 1:55
Period 6   2:00 – 2:55

TUNING IN.

Look at the clocks. Listen to the students. Point to each clock that shows the time you hear.

TALKING IT OVER. What time is it?

Unit 1

FIGURING IT OUT. Tell the time on each watch. What period is it at Kennedy? Check the bell schedule to find out.

ON YOUR OWN. Draw a clock to show each time. Write the time under each clock, using *numbers*.

1. nine o'clock
2. ten o'clock
3. two o'clock
4. four o'clock
5. ten-fifteen
6. two-fifteen
7. four-ten
8. five past twelve
9. four-thirty
10. five-thirty
11. (a) quarter to eleven
12. ten to two
13. one forty-five
14. five after twelve
15. five to twelve
16. ten to eight

LISTENING IN. Does Juan like basketball?

Chip: We have an after-school sports program. Here's our sports calendar.
Juan: I don't understand.
Chip: Do you like sports? Sports. You know basketball . . . dribble, dribble . . . shoot . . . basketball.
Juan: Oh! Basketball. I like basketball!

READING ALOUD.

Look at the calendar. First name the days of the week. Then name each sport on the calendar.

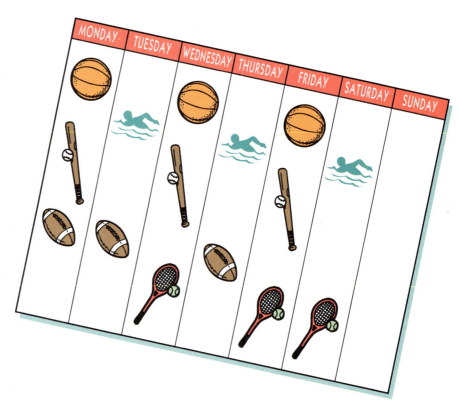

TALKING IT OVER. Name a sport that you like.

 Play a guessing game.
▲ Think of a sport.
▲ Use actions to tell about the sport.
Can your classmates guess the sport?

8   Unit 1

UNIT 2
YOU'LL MAKE A LOT OF FRIENDS!

TUNING IN. Look at the picture. Listen to the conversation.

Now listen one more time. Point to the person who is speaking.

Lori: Hi, Chip! How's it going?
Chip: Pretty good! Do you know Juan Ortíz?
Lori: No, I don't.
Chip: Juan . . . Lori! Lori . . . Juan! Juan's new here!
Juan: Hi.
Lori: Glad to meet you! You'll like it here at Kennedy. There's a lot to do.
Chip: And a lot of neat kids! . . . Hey, there's Shelley! Hey, Shelley!

Unit 2   9

READING ALONG. Read about some of the students at Kennedy.

More than 900 students attend Kennedy Middle School.

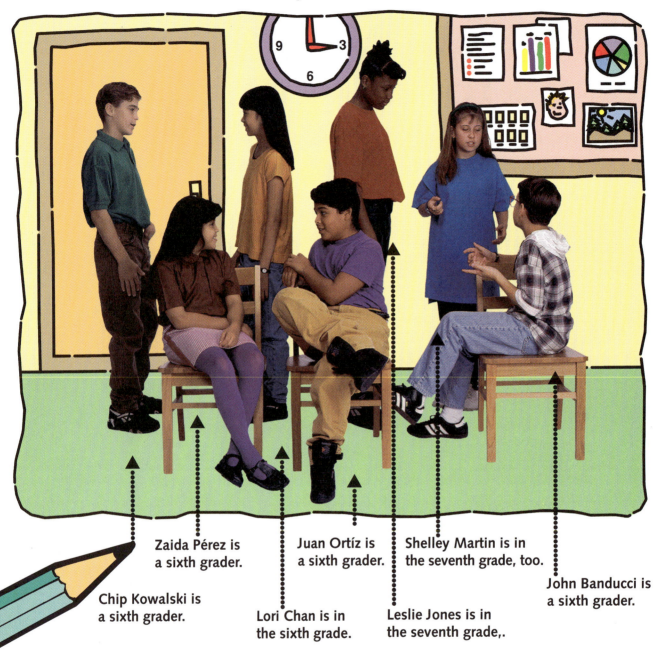

Chip Kowalski is a sixth grader.
Zaida Pérez is a sixth grader.
Lori Chan is in the sixth grade.
Juan Ortíz is a sixth grader.
Leslie Jones is in the seventh grade,.
Shelley Martin is in the seventh grade, too.
John Banducci is a sixth grader.

ACTING IT OUT. Try these short conversations with your classmates.

1. **Chip:** I'm in the sixth grade!
   Lori: So am I. We're both sixth graders.

2. **Zaida:** He's a sixth grader.
   Juan: She's in the sixth grade, too.

3. **Leslie:** You're a seventh grader, aren't you?
   Shelley: Yes, I'm a seventh grader.
   John: They're both seventh graders. I'm only a sixth grader.

FOLLOWING ALONG. Make a new friend! Follow these instructions with a classmate.

1. Walk toward each other.

2. Put out your right hand.

3. Look at each other in the eyes. Smile.

4. Shake hands.

Hi, my name is Chip Kowalski!

Glad to meet you. I'm Juan Ortíz. I'm a sixth grader.

5. Introduce yourself.

TUNING IN. Look at the students' pictures on page 10. Listen as they introduce themselves. Finish each student's sentence.

TALKING IT OVER. Introduce yourself to your classmates.

ACTING IT OUT. Try this conversation with a partner.

Chip: Do you like football?
Lori: Yes, I do.
Chip: Me, too! Do you like wrestling?
Lori: No, I don't. What about you?
Chip: I love wrestling!
Lori: Do you like volleyball?
Chip: Not much. What about you?
Lori: Me, neither!

I like basketball.

So do I!

WRITING AND SHARING. Friends often share the same *likes* and *dislikes*. Make a chart like this one that shows the sports that you like and the sports that you don't like. Share your chart with a classmate. Then find someone who likes the same sports that you do.

Sports that I like...   Sports that I don't like...

🎧 **TUNING IN.** Listen to some questions about sports. Point your thumb up if you like the sport. Point your thumb down if you don't like the sport.

Do you like softball?

TALKING IT OVER. Talk with a partner about sports. Share your likes and dislikes.

I like volleyball!

I don't like wrestling!

Make a collage! Cut and paste pictures from magazines and newspapers that show things you like to do. Share your collage with your classmates.

ACTING IT OUT. Try this conversation with a partner.

Chip: It's raining! We can't go out. What do you want to do?
Juan: I don't know.
Chip: Well, what do you like to do?
Juan: I like playing computer games!
Chip: Me, too. Let's play!
Juan: OK!

READING AND SHARING.

Read the list of rainy day activities. Tell your classmates which activities you like and which you don't like.

Rainy day activities
1. play a board game
2. bake cookies
3. work on a puzzle
4. clean up room
5. read magazines
6. sew
7. work on a model airplane
8. talk on the phone
9. write letters to friends
10. listen to music

I like baking cookies.

WRITING AND SHARING. Write the activities on the list in order—from your favorite to your least favorite. Then share your list with a classmate.

Bring something to class that shows what you like to do for fun. For example, you could bring in a book or something you've made. Have a "Show and Tell" with your classmates.

LISTENING IN. What are Chip and Juan going to make?

Let's have lunch. I'll make tuna sandwiches. You can help me.

Sure! I'm hungry.

TUNING IN. Listen to the conversation. Point to the picture that matches what you hear.

a. mixing bowl
b. tuna
c. bread
d. mixing the tuna and the mayo
e. can opener
f. milk
g. slicing sandwiches
h. lettuce
i. plates and napkins

ACTING IT OUT. Show your classmates how to make something to eat. Use real objects or pictures.

Unit 2   15

ACTING IT OUT. Try this conversation with a partner. Then try it again with the names of other students from the yearbook.

Chip: Want to see our yearbook?
Juan: What's a yearbook?
Chip: It's a book with pictures of all the students in our school. I'll show you . . . Here I am. And here's Lori. You know Lori?
Juan: Yes, I do. I like her. She's nice.
Chip: And here's George Martinez.
Juan: Do you like him?
Chip: Oh, I guess so. And here are the Johnson twins.
Juan: Do you like them?
Chip: Well . . . we call them double trouble!

Lori Chan   Alex Johnson   Andrew Johnson

Amy Kim   Chip Kowalski   Diane Lee

Becky Lipton   George Martinez   Anna Moreno

Make your own class yearbook. Put everyone's picture and name in the correct order.

I'M TAKING ESL!

TUNING IN. Look at the picture. Listen to the conversation.

Now listen one more time. Point to the person who is speaking.

Ms. Reed: Hello there!
Juan: Is this ESL?
Ms. Reed: Yes, it is! May I see your class schedule?
Juan: Class schedule?
Ms. Reed: Yes, your class schedule. You have it in your hand.
Juan: This?
Ms. Reed: Yes. That's it. . . . Students, this is Juan Ortíz. Sit over there, next to Neelam.
Juan: Thank you.

READING ALONG. Meet the students in Juan's ESL class.

Neelam is sitting next to Roberto.

Nina is sitting between Rama and Carlos.

Raul and Miyako are sitting at the back of the room.

Rama is sitting behind Roberto.

Sit over there, next to Neelam.

Juan is standing next to Ms. Reed.

Susana is sitting in front of Tomás.

Maria is sitting near Ms. Reed.

Renato is sitting in front of Tran.

FIGURING IT OUT. Read each clue. Name the students.

1. She is sitting next to Raul.
2. She is sitting next to Nina.
3. He is sitting in front of Rama.
4. She is sitting between Renato and Susana.
5. He is sitting behind Susana.
6. They are sitting in the front row.
7. She's sitting near Maria.
8. He is standing next to Ms. Reed.
9. He is sitting between Tran and Rama.
10. She's sitting in front of Nina.

18 Unit 3

TUNING IN. Look at the picture. Listen to Ms. Reed. Follow her directions.

READING ALOUD. Name the objects.

FOLLOWING ALONG.

Follow your teacher's directions.

Unit 3   19

READING ALOUD. Read the heading.

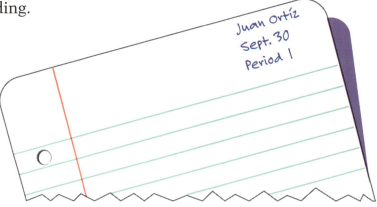

You need to learn how to head your assignments.

FOLLOWING ALONG. Write a heading. Follow these steps.

▲ Take out a piece of paper.

▲ Take a pencil or pen.

▲ Write your name in the upper right-hand corner. Follow this order: Write your first name. Then write your last name.

▲ Next write the date under your name.

▲ Now write the class period under the date.

READING ALONG.

Read about the Kennedy mascot.

Kennedy Middle School has a *mascot*. Kennedy's mascot is a cougar. The Kennedy Cougar is on the front of every school notebook and book cover.

You'll need a school notebook for your work. Our mascot is on the cover.

TALKING IT OVER.

Does your school have a mascot? What is it?

Make a list of the places at school where you can find pictures of your school mascot.

20   Unit 3

READING ALONG. Read the classroom rules.

We have some simple classroom rules. The rules are posted on the bulletin board.

Our Classroom Rules
* Be on time
  1st Tardy: Warning
  2nd Tardy: Detention
  3rd Tardy: Go to the counselor's office.
* Listen to the teacher and to other students.
* Raise your hand when you want to talk or ask a question.
* Come to class ready to work. Bring your books and supplies.
* Remember, everyone has the right to learn! You may not prevent others from learning.

TALKING IT OVER.

What are the rules in your ESL class? What are the rules in your other classes? Are the rules the same in all your classes?

WRITING AND SHARING.

Add more rules to Ms. Reed's list. Share them with your classmates.

No gum in class!

TUNING IN. Listen to Ms. Reed's classroom rules. For each rule, point your thumb up if it is one of your classroom rules. Point your thumb down if it is not one of your classroom rules.

LISTENING IN. What are Juan and Tran doing? What are they talking about?

"In my class, you'll often work with others. Sometimes you'll work with a partner. And sometimes you'll work in small groups."

Juan: I like hot dogs. Do you?
Tran: No!
Juan: And I like hamburgers.
Tran: So do I! I love cheeseburgers! Do you?
Juan: No, I don't. I like plain hamburgers.

TUNING IN.

Juan and Tran are making a diagram that shows the foods they like. Listen to their conversation. Where should they write the name of each food? Point to the correct place in the diagram.

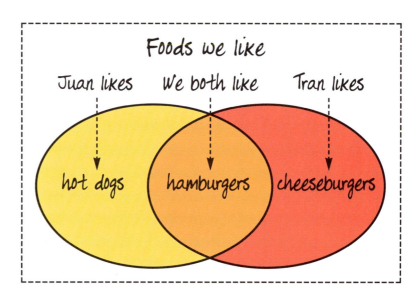

Foods we like
Juan likes — We both like — Tran likes
hot dogs — hamburgers — cheeseburgers

WRITING AND SHARING. Work with a partner. Make a Venn diagram that shows the foods you like. Share your diagram with your classmates.

22   Unit 3

FIGURING IT OUT. What are the students doing?

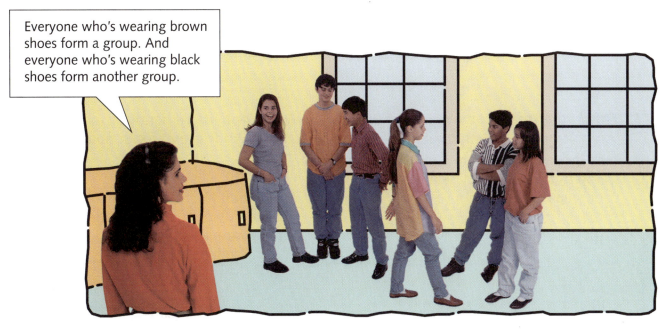

What are the students doing now?

TALKING IT OVER.

What are some other ways to form small groups?

Unit 3   23

FIGURING IT OUT. What are the students doing?

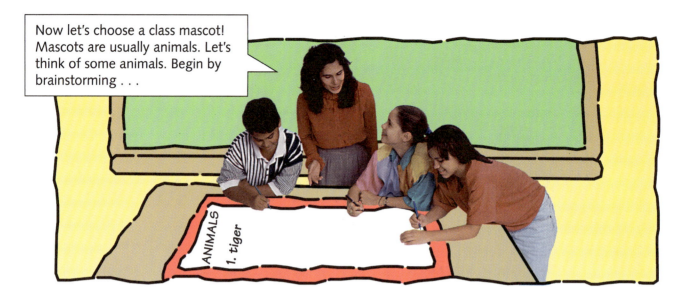

"Now let's choose a class mascot! Mascots are usually animals. Let's think of some animals. Begin by brainstorming . . ."

 Choose your own class mascot. Follow these steps.

1. **Think about it.** In small groups, brainstorm a list of animals.
2. **Talk it over.** Which animal do you think would make the best class mascot? In your small group, take a vote.
3. **Draw and share.** Draw a picture of the mascot your group likes. Share it with the other groups. Talk about the choices for class mascot.
4. **Make a choice.** Which animal do you think would make the best mascot? With your classmates, take a vote.

24 Unit 3

UNIT 4

I LIKE MY MORNING CLASSES!

TUNING IN.

Look at the picture and the school map. Listen to the conversation.

Now listen one more time. Trace Chip's directions on the school map.

Chip: What's your next class?
Juan: PE.
Chip: That's in the gym.
Juan: Where's the gym?
Chip: Look at your map. Here we are, in front of room 3. Go down the hall to the foyer. Turn left. Go outside. Go across the quad. Find the door that says Boys Locker Room.
Juan: Thanks.

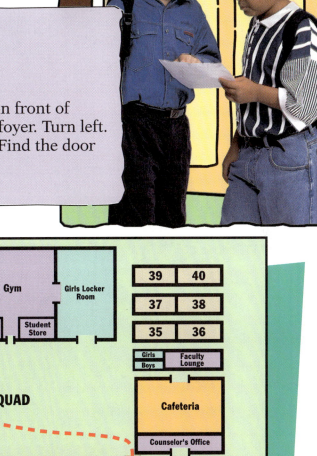

John F. Kennedy Middle School

ACTING IT OUT. What are the students doing? Try it with your classmates.

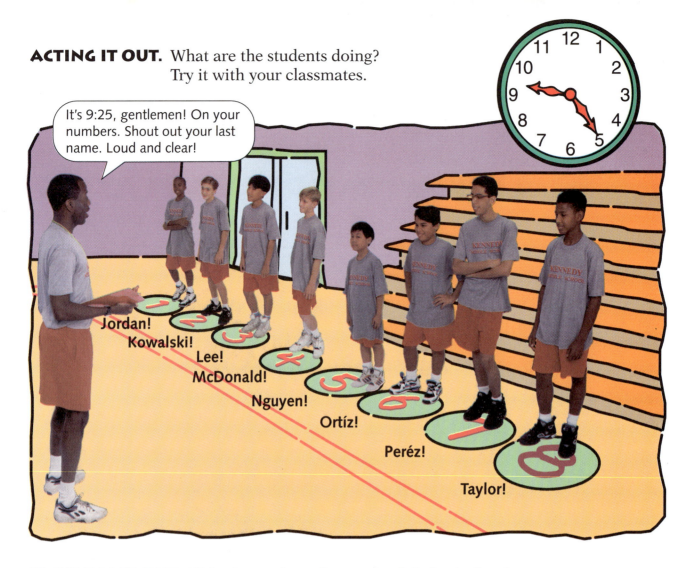

FIGURING IT OUT. Help the students line up in alphabetical order.

ON YOUR OWN. Bring something from home that is organized in alphabetical order. Share it with your classmates.

26   Unit 4

TUNING IN.

Listen to Juan and Chip's conversation. For each sport that you hear, point your thumb up if Juan likes the sport. Point your thumb down if he doesn't like it.

TALKING IT OVER.

Talk with your classmates. Tell which sports you like and which you don't like.

a. baseball

b. hockey

c. swimming

d. track

e. badminton

f. basketball

FINDING OUT.

Work with a group of classmates whose favorite team sport is the same as yours. How many players are on the team? What kind of equipment do the players use? Do the players wear uniforms or special clothing? Make a poster or chart. Be ready to share what you've learned with the other groups.

g. tumbling

Unit 4   27

READING ALOUD. Name the art materials.

Welcome to art class! Let me show you some of the materials and supplies you'll be using for drawing and painting.

a. pencils

b. pen and ink

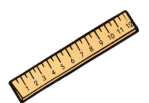
c. crayons

d. ruler

e. markers

f. brushes

g. paper towels

h. watercolors

i. water

j. butcher paper

k. paste

l. drawing paper

m. clay

n. X-acto® knife

FOLLOWING ALONG. Draw a self-portrait! Follow the directions.

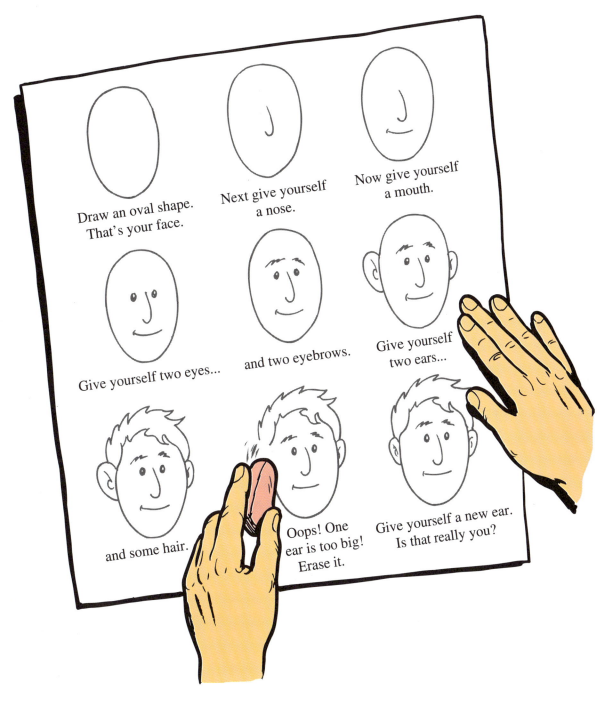

TUNING IN. Draw a silly portrait! Listen and follow the directions.

JUST FOR Fun — Draw a portrait of yourself at age five. Next draw a portrait of yourself as you look today. Finally draw a portrait of yourself as an adult. Share your portraits with your classmates.

FIGURING IT OUT. Look at the timeline. Talk about it with your classmates.

Welcome to social studies. This year in world history we're going to study ancient civilizations. Now we're working on a timeline.

I see.

READING ALONG.

Read about different writing systems.

A.

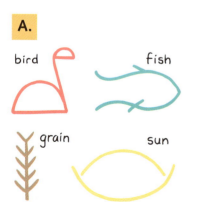

The Sumerians invented the first writing system. They used word-pictures.

B.

About 3000 B.C. the Sumerians started to use symbols that were made up of wedges — tiny marks shaped like triangles. They used about 600 symbols. They wrote with a special tool called a stylus.

30 Unit 4

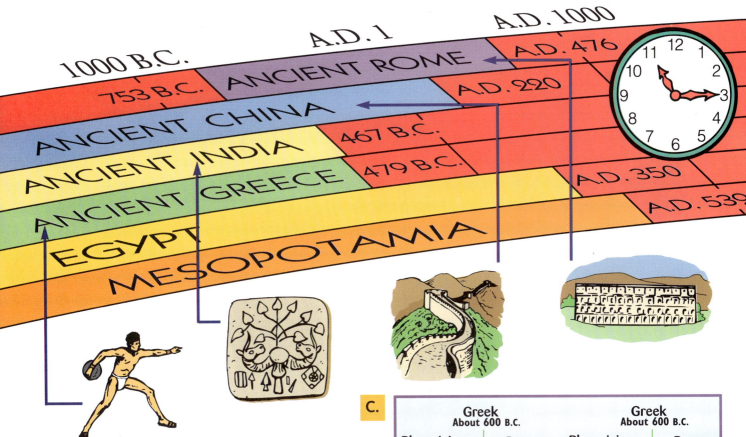

About 900 B.C. the Phoenicians invented an alphabet with 22 letters.

Later the Greeks borrowed the symbols from the Phoenician alphabet. They used them to form their own alphabet.

Then the Romans borrowed the Greek alphabet! They changed the symbols a little to fit their language.

Many languages, such as English, use alphabets based on the Roman alphabet.

🎧 TUNING IN.

First listen to the list of letters. Print each letter. Then listen to Juan and his friends spell their names. Print each name.

Work with a partner. Invent a writing system that uses pictures. Then write a simple message for classmates to decipher.

READING ALOUD. Read the lunch menu.

Juan! Let's eat in the cafeteria!

OK.

Menu

Group 1: ENTREES

Burrito	1.35
BBQ Chicken Sandwich	2.10
Chicken Pattie on a Bun	1.95
Cold Sandwich on White or Whole Wheat	2.25
Hamburger on a Bun	1.50
Cheeseburger on a Bun	1.75
Hot Dog on a Bun	.75
Hot Pastrami & Cheese on Rye	2.50
Ham & Turkey Melt on Toast	2.50
Hot Ham & Cheese on a Croissant	2.35
Pepperoni Pizza	1.50
Tostizza (Mexican Pizza)	1.90

DAILY SPECIALS

Monday	Torpedo Submarine	2.50
Tuesday	Macaroni & Cheese w/Ham	2.50
Wednesday	Chicken Chow Mein	2.50
Thursday	Super Burrito	2.50
Friday	Taco Salad	2.50

Group 2: FRUIT

Fresh Fruit in Season	.45
Chilled Fruit Cup	.45
Frozen Fruit Shape-up	.75
Fruit Juice (4 oz.)	.50

Grape, Apple, Orange, Pineapple Orange, or Fruit Punch

Group 3: VEGETABLES

Tossed Green Salad	1.50
Hot Vegetable of the Day	1.15
French Fries	1.25

Group 4: MILK/DAIRY

Low Fat Milk	.30
Whole Milk	.25
Chocolate Milk	.30

FOLLOWING ALONG. It's time for lunch! Follow the directions.

- ▲ Get in line.
- ▲ Take a tray.
- ▲ Take some utensils.
- ▲ Take a green salad.
- ▲ Take a sandwich.
- ▲ Take a bag of potato chips.
- ▲ Take a piece of pie.
- ▲ Take a carton of milk.
- ▲ Don't forget a straw!
- ▲ Take out your wallet.
- ▲ Hand the cashier some money.
- ▲ Hold out your hand for the change.
- ▲ Put the change in your pocket.

I LIKE MY AFTERNOON CLASSES, TOO!

TUNING IN. Look at the map. Listen to the conversation.

Now listen one more time. As Chip gives Juan directions, trace the route on the school map.

Chip: There's the bell! What's your next class?
Juan: Math.
Chip: Who's your teacher?
Juan: Mrs. Delgado.
Chip: Oh. I think she's in room 23.
Juan: Where's room 23?
Chip: Get out your map. OK, we're right here, in the cafeteria. Go outside. Then go . . .

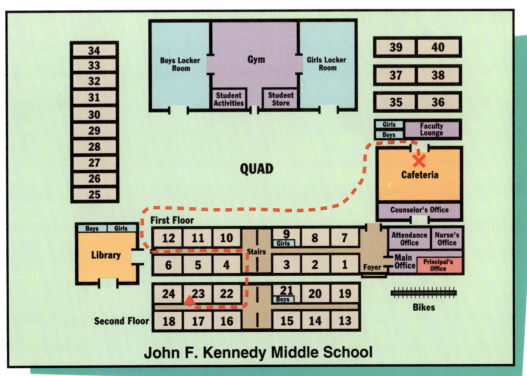

Unit 5   33

FIGURING IT OUT. What is the class doing?

Let's play some math games! This game is called Target Addition. Work with a partner. Here is the game board. You'll each need some colored markers.

TUNING IN. Listen to the tape. As Mrs. Delgado asks each question, say the answer aloud. Then write the answer down.

5 plus 4 is 9.

PLAYING A GAME. Play Target Addition with a partner. Follow the rules.

1. Each pair of students chooses a "winning number" between 25 and 55. Write the winning number on a piece of paper.

2. Decide who goes first, and then take turns placing a marker on a number.

3. Each student must add up his or her covered numbers on each turn.

4. Put only one marker on each square.

5. The first player to reach the winning number *exactly* wins! If a player goes over the winning number, he or she loses.

LISTENING IN. What is the next game called?

A = $ 1	N = $14
B = $ 2	O = $15
C = $ 3	P = $16
D = $ 4	Q = $17
E = $ 5	R = $18
F = $ 6	S = $19
G = $ 7	T = $20
H = $ 8	U = $21
I = $ 9	V = $22
J = $10	W = $23
K = $11	X = $24
L = $12	Y = $25
M = $13	Z = $26

The next game is fun. It's called Word Value. Look at the chart. How much is each letter in your name worth? Add the letter values.

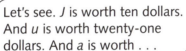

Let's see. *J* is worth ten dollars. And *u* is worth twenty-one dollars. And *a* is worth . . .

PLAYING A GAME. Play Word Value with your classmates.

1. How much is Juan's first name worth?
2. What is Juan's last name? How much is it worth?
3. How much are your first and last names worth?
4. What is the difference between the value of your first name and your last name?
5. Who has the most valuable first name in your class?
6. Who has the least valuable first name?
7. Now try multiplying the letter values in your first name.

1. Find the most expensive object in your classroom.
2. Look through a book or magazine for the most expensive word that you can find. How much is it worth? Share your word with your classmates. Who found the most expensive word?

FIGURING IT OUT.

How do you play this game?

I'm going to give each of you some play money and a coin board. You're going to go shopping in the student store. I want you to figure out how many different ways you could pay for each item that you're going to buy. Show each way — by placing the coins in the rows on your coin boards.

READING ALOUD. Read the price tags.

Each item here costs ninety-nine cents or less.

TUNING IN. Listen to the store clerk. Write the amount you hear.

READING ALOUD. Read the labels in the chart.

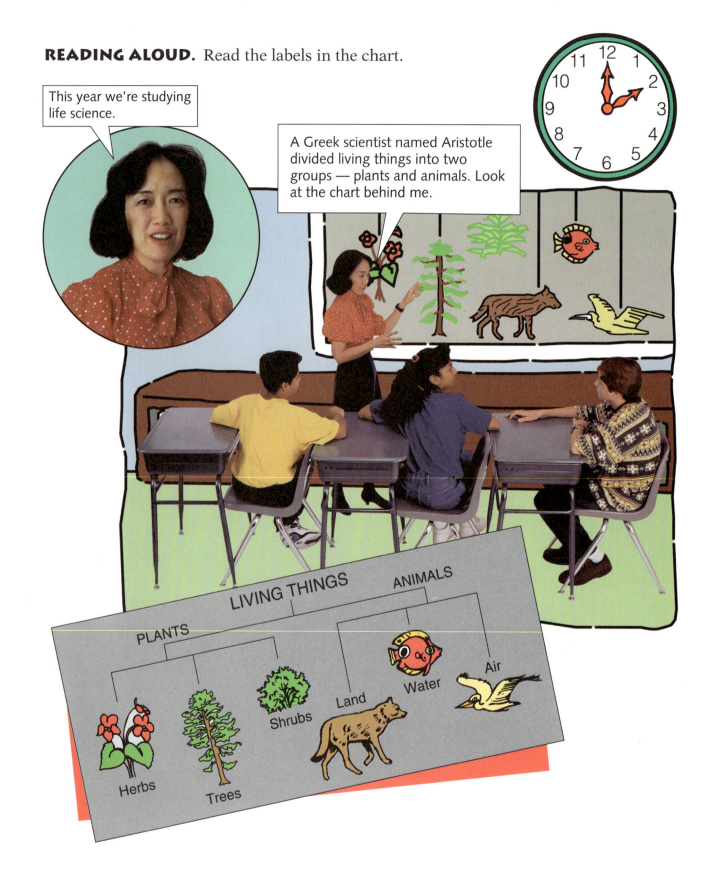

"This year we're studying life science."

"A Greek scientist named Aristotle divided living things into two groups — plants and animals. Look at the chart behind me."

TUNING IN. Listen to Ms. Yoshida-Johnson. Hold up one finger when you hear the name of a plant. Hold up two fingers when you hear the name of an animal.

38 Unit 5

TALKING IT OVER. Name the living things in this picture.

FIGURING IT OUT.

Make a chart like this one. Tell which living things are plants and which living things are animals.

PLANTS	ANIMALS

Make your own chart. Clip pictures of plants and animals from magazines. Paste each picture in the correct place and label it. Share your chart with your classmates.

Unit 5   39

READING ALONG. Read more about living things.

"What do you know about living things? What do all living things do?"

Living things come from other living things.

Living things move.

Living things breathe and eat.

Living things grow and living things die.

FINDING OUT. Work with your classmates. Make an animal atlas. Include animals that walk, fly, swim, and slither. Learn where each animal in your atlas lives, what each animal eats, and how long each animal lives.

ARE YOU READY TO WORK?

TUNING IN. Look at the picture. Listen to the students.

Now listen one more time. Point to the student who is speaking.

LISTENING IN.

Why is Maria late?

Ms. Reed: It's 8:25, Maria. You're ten minutes late.
Maria: I'm sorry. My locker wouldn't open.
Ms. Reed: This is your third tardy. Go see Ms. Vasquez. Here's a hall pass.

READING ALOUD.

Read the information on the hall pass.

Your locker wouldn't open? That's not a good excuse!

HALL PASS
KENNEDY MIDDLE SCHOOL

Name: Maria de la Ossa Grade: 6
Date: 10/3
Pass to: Time: 8:25
Room # ____ Locker # ____
Lavatory — Library — Office ✓
Errand: ____
Misconduct: 3rd tardy

Ms. Reed
Teacher's Signature

TALKING IT OVER.

Read the common excuses for being late. Which ones are good excuses? Which ones are poor excuses? Talk with your classmates.

I had to go to the bathroom!

I felt sick!

I was talking with my friends.

I forgot my books!

My locker wouldn't open!

I didn't hear the bell ring!

ACTING IT OUT. Try this conversation with a partner.

Zaida: It's almost 10:15. I need to go to class now. I don't want to be late!
Chip: Oh, you're right! I need to go, too. I'm never late!

TUNING IN.

First make a chart like the one here. Then listen and fill in your chart. Is each student on time or late for class? Check the bell schedule.

BELL SCHEDULE

Period 1	8:15– 9:10
Period 2	9:15–10:10
Period 3	10:15–11:10
Period 4	11:15–12:10
Lunch	12:10–12:50
Period 5	1:00– 1:55
Period 6	2:00– 2:55

Student	Period	Time
1. Zaida		
2. Tran		
3. Leslie		
4. Chip		
5. Shelley		
6. Juan		
7. Neelam		

JUST FOR Fun

Make a log for one school day. Record the exact time you get to each of your classes. Were you on time to every class? Compare your log with your classmates' logs.

Unit 6   43

"You can all do well in school. Here's a checklist of things that good students do."

READING ALOUD. Read the checklist.

ARE YOU ALWAYS READY TO WORK?

Check the things that you always do.

- ❏ I'm in my seat when the bell rings.
- ❏ I bring a pen or pencil to class.
- ❏ I bring my books to class.
- ❏ I bring my homework to class.
- ❏ I listen to others.
- ❏ I raise my hand when I have a question.
- ❏ _____
- ❏ _____
- ❏ _____
- ❏ _____
- ❏ _____
- ❏ _____
- ❏ _____

TUNING IN.

Listen as Ms. Reed reviews the checklist. Point your thumb up for the things that you always do. Point your thumb down for the things that you don't always do.

THINKING ABOUT IT.

Think of other items to add to the checklist.

TALKING IT OVER.

Ask and answer with a partner.

1. Are you always in your seat when the bell rings?
2. Do you always remember to bring a pen or pencil to class?
3. Do you always remember your books?
4. Do you always remember your notebook?
5. Do you always remember your homework?

FOLLOWING ALONG. Make a notebook. Follow the directions.

You need to keep a notebook. Here's how to organize it.

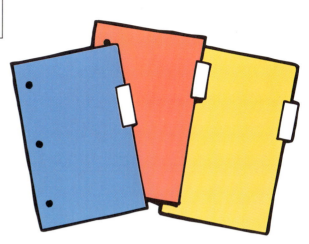

1. First you need to make dividers with tabs.

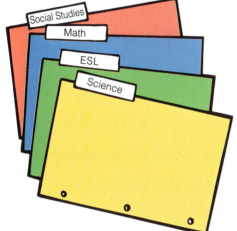

2. Make a tab for each subject you're taking.

Time	Monday	Tuesday	Wednesday	Thursday	Friday
4:00–5:00					
5:00–6:00					
6:00–7:00					
7:00–8:00					
8:00–9:00					

3. Make a section for your homework schedules.

SUBJECT	MONDAY	TUESDAY	WEDNESDAY	THURSDAY	FRIDAY
ESL					
MATH					
SCIENCE					
SOCIAL STUDIES					
—					
—					

4. Make a section for your assignment sheets.

5. Keep your notes, tests, and homework in your notebook.

"It's important to do your homework. Write down your homework assignments each day on your assignment sheet."

READING ALOUD.

Read the homework assignments.

SUBJECT	MONDAY	TUESDAY	WEDNESDAY	THURSDAY	FRIDAY
ESL	Portfolio p. 16	Bring in picture of family.	Portfolio p. 17		
MATH	p. 40, problems 1-8				
SCIENCE				Study for quiz.	
SOCIAL STUDIES		Read Chapter 3, pp. 72-76.			Watch "Washington: Week in Review"
___					
___					

ON YOUR OWN. Make a list of the materials you need to bring home from school so that you can do your homework. Share your list with a partner. Did you remember everything?

46   Unit 6

READING ALOUD. Juan does his homework in his bedroom. He has everything he needs at his desk. Name each item.

It's important that you have a place to do your homework.

📼 **TUNING IN.**

Point to each item that Juan names.

WRITING AND SHARING. Make a schedule like this one. Show

▲ what you do after school.   ▲ when you eat dinner.   ▲ what you do after dinner.

Share your schedule with your classmates. Do you spend enough time on your homework?

Time	Monday	Tuesday	Wednesday	Thursday	Friday
4:00–5:00					
5:00–6:00					
6:00–7:00					
7:00–8:00					
8:00–9:00					

Unit 6

LISTENING IN.

Who is the Student of the Week?

Ms. Reed: Each week I'll choose one of you to be Student of the Week. The Student of the Week is a good student who follows all the classroom rules. This week's award goes to Neelam Singh!
Neelam: Thank you very much!

READING ALONG.

Read why Neelam is Student of the Week.

Neelam is always on time. She always brings her books to class. She always remembers her homework. She always listens to others.

FINDING OUT.

Which students in your class deserve a turn to be Student of the Week? Find out.

Student of the Week
Name: Neelam Singh
Date: October 23 - 27
Awarded by: Ms. Reed

Find someone who . . .	Name
listens to others.	
did his or her homework last night.	
is always on time for class.	
enjoys studying.	
keeps all of his or her work in a notebook.	
always brings his or her books to class.	

JUST FOR Fun

Work in a small group. Design your own certificate. Award the certificate to a classmate in another group.

LET'S CALL YOUR UNCLE!

TUNING IN. Look at the picture. Listen to the conversation.

Now listen one more time. Use your hand and face to show how Juan feels.

Mrs. Smith:	Juan! You look terrible! Do you feel OK?
Juan:	I feel sick.
Mrs. Smith:	You'd better go home. Let me call your uncle. Where can I reach him?
Juan:	He's at work.
Mrs. Smith:	Do you know his work number, or should I check your emergency card?
Juan:	Uh . . . 555-8921.
Mrs. Smith:	You can wait on the bench, dear. Let me feel your forehead.

Unit 7 49

TALKING IT OVER. What's your telephone number? Ask and answer with a partner.

"What's your home phone number?"

"555-6561."

"Area code 201-555-2047."

"We don't have a phone."

"Give me the number. I'll push the buttons."

TUNING IN. As you hear each telephone number, point to the correct buttons on the telephone.

ON YOUR OWN. Make a list of people that your school could call if you have an emergency. Find out the daytime phone number for each person.

LISTENING IN. What's wrong with each student?

Mrs. Park: Are you all waiting to see me? What's wrong with you, Lori?
Lori: I have a headache.
Mrs. Park: And what's wrong with you, Shelley?
Shelley: I feel sick to my stomach.
Mrs. Park: And what's wrong with you, Chip?
Chip: My foot hurts.

ACTING IT OUT. First try the conversation with your classmates. Then look at the pictures. Practice telling the school nurse what's wrong with you.

toothache   headache   sprained ankle   backache

earache   stomachache   head cold

Write a get-well card to a friend or family member.

Unit 7   51

ACTING IT OUT.

Try this conversation with a partner.

Ms. Reed: Juan! How do you feel?
Juan: Much better, thank you.
Ms. Reed: Do you have a pass?
Juan: Here's a note.
Ms. Reed: No, no . . . You have to take your note to the attendance office. The attendance clerk will give you a pass.
Juan: Oh, I understand.

READING ALOUD.

Read the note.

October 31

To Whom It May Concern:

Please excuse my nephew, Juan Ortiz, for his absence the past three days. He had a bad cold. Thank you for your consideration.

Sincerely,
Carlos Ortiz
555-8921

TUNING IN.

Pretend that you have been out sick. Tell your teacher what was wrong with you. Answer each question.

I had a headache.

I felt sick to my stomach.

I hurt my foot.

TALKING IT OVER. Here are some common problems that you might have at school. Do you know what to do? Do you know where to go? Do you know who can help you? Talk with your classmates.

You feel sick.

You're late for school.

You lose your book.

You lose your lunch money.

You've been absent from school.

Your locker won't open.

You forget your lunch money.

Somebody shoves or hits you.

Unit 7   53

LISTENING IN. Where is the ESL class going?

Ms. Reed: I'm glad you feel better, Juan. You wouldn't want to miss our field trip on Friday!
Juan: Where are we going?
Ms. Reed: To the zoo.
Neelam: Ms. Reed, do you want our field-trip permission forms?
Ms. Reed: Thank you for reminding me, Neelam! Remember, class, you need to turn in your permission forms by tomorrow.
Juan: What form is it?
Ms. Reed: It's the field-trip permission form. This is what it looks like. Your uncle needs to sign it.

READING ALONG.

Read the permission form.

FIELD-TRIP PERMISSION FORM

The _____ESL 1_____ at Kennedy Middle
(class or club)
School will visit _____Brookview Zoo_____
(place)
on _____November 2_____.
(date)
We will leave at _____9:00 A.M._____ and will return to
(time)
school at _____2:45 P.M._____.
(time)
Transportation will be provided by: _____Reliable Bus Co._____
Cost: _____$3.50_____   Food: _____Bring lunch_____

I give _____Juan Ortiz_____ permission to
(name)
participate in this field trip.

_____Carlos Ortiz_____
(parent or guardian)
_____October 31_____   _____555-8921_____
(date)   (phone number)

54   Unit 7

TUNING IN. Listen as Juan answers Uncle Carlos's questions. Point to the picture that matches Juan's words.

"You're going on a field trip? Where are you going? How are you getting there?"

a. to the zoo
b. to the museum
c. to the aquarium
d. to City Hall
e. to a play

TALKING IT OVER. Work in a small group. Plan your own field trip.

f. on the bus
g. by car
h. by foot
i. on the subway

▲ Make a list of places in your community that you might visit.

▲ Decide where you will go.

▲ Discuss how you will get there, and how long the trip will take.

▲ Find out how much the trip will cost.

Organize the information in a chart like the one below. Share your chart with other groups.

FIELD TRIPS			
Place	Transportation	Cost	Time

Unit 7   55

READING ALONG. Read the school notices.

"Here are other kinds of information that you might take home."

John F. Kennedy Middle School
BACK-TO-SCHOOL NIGHT

COME VISIT OUR SCHOOL!

September 11

DATE: 9/11   TIME: 7:00 P.M.

It is very important! Please come! Meet the teachers!

John F. Kennedy Middle School
PARENT-TEACHER CONFERENCE

Please come to school to meet with _Juan_ 's teacher.

November 30

DATE: 11/30   TIME: 7:30 P.M.   PLACE: Room 10

Please complete and return the teacher.

Carlos Ortiz will meet with the teacher on _11/30_ at _7:30 P.M._ o'clock.
       Date   Time

☐ Check here if you need schedule another appointment.

Carlos Ortiz   _555-8921_
Parent/Guardian Signature   Phone Number

John F. Kennedy Middle School
SCHOOL RULES

I have spoken to _Juan Ortiz_ about the school rules for attendance and behavior. I explained the punishment for breaking the school rules.

Carlos Ortiz
Parent/Guardian Signature

I understand and promise to obey the school rules.

Juan Ortiz
Student Signature

ON YOUR OWN. Bring home a notice or form from school. Explain it to your parents or other adult members of your family.

UNIT 8
THIS IS OUR STUDENT HANDBOOK!

TUNING IN. Look at the picture. Listen to the conversation.

Now listen again and point to the person who is talking.

Chip:	Excuse me, but my friend doesn't have a locker.
Juan:	Yes, I need a locker, Mrs. Smith.
Mrs. Smith:	You'll need to supply your own combination lock.
Juan:	I have a lock. Here it is.
Mrs. Smith:	Fine. I'll assign you a locker.
Juan:	Thank you.
Mrs. Smith:	We have locker rules at Kennedy. They're printed in the Student Handbook. Here's a copy.
Chip:	I'll explain what everything means. I'll explain all our school rules.
Juan:	Let's find my locker first!

READING ALONG.

Read the locker rules.

Locker Rules

1. Go to the main office for a locker assignment.
2. Provide your own combination lock.
3. Memorize your combination.
4. Keep your locker clean and organized.
5. Do not share your locker.

Help John clean his locker. Which things belong in his locker? Which things should he take home? Which things should he throw away? Work with a partner. Make a chart.

▶ **TUNING IN.** Listen to Juan as he opens his locker.

I'd better practice opening my locker. My combination is 10-20-44.

Unit 8

"Kennedy has a dress code. Here are the rules."

READING ALONG.

Read the rules in the dress code.

Kennedy Dress Code

1. No bare feet. Students must wear shoes.
2. No undershirts without shirts over them.
3. No cutoffs.
4. No halter tops or net T-shirts.
5. No hats on in the school building.
6. No shorts.
7. No T-shirts with offensive words.
8. No curlers or rollers.

TUNING IN. Is Kennedy's dress code fair? Listen as Chip reads each rule to Juan. Point your thumb up if you think the rule is fair. Point your thumb down if you think the rule is unfair.

WRITING AND SHARING. Does your school have a dress code? If so, write down each rule. Talk with your classmates. Compare your school's dress code to Kennedy's dress code.

TUNING IN.

Listen as Lori and Chip decide what they'll wear to school. Look at their closets. Point to each item of clothing that they choose.

I'll wear my blue skirt.

. . . and my baseball cap.

Unit 8

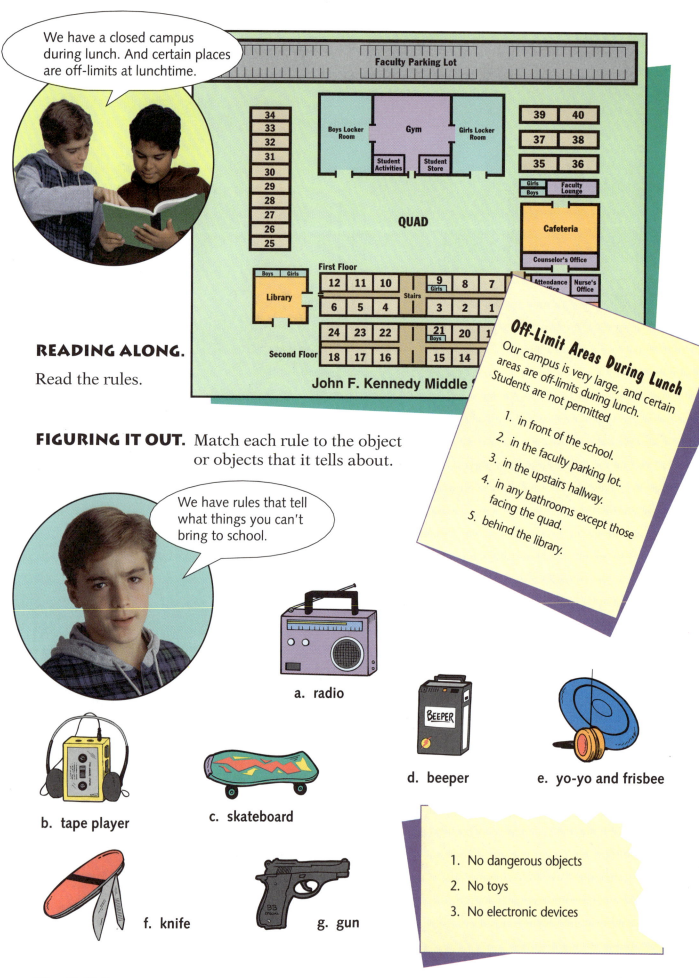

READING ALONG.

Read the rules.

FIGURING IT OUT. Match each rule to the object or objects that it tells about.

LISTENING IN.

What is Kennedy Cash?

Chip: If you follow the rules, you can earn Kennedy Cash.
Juan: What's Kennedy Cash?
Chip: It looks like this. Teachers give it to you when you're good. You can buy things with Kennedy Cash. The more good things you do, the more cash you can earn.

FIGURING IT OUT.

Look at the pictures. What are some ways that students can earn Kennedy Cash?

You can earn Kennedy Cash if . . .

. . . you're on time to class.

. . . you help clean up school grounds.

. . . you help a teacher.

Work with a partner. Make a poster that shows how to earn Kennedy Cash. Write "How to Earn Kennedy Cash" at the top of the poster. Decide how many *greenbacks* each good deed will earn.

READING ALONG. Read the bus rules.

Bus Rules
1. Line up in an orderly manner.
2. Remain seated while the bus is in motion.
3. No pushing or shoving.
4. No food or drinks.
5. Treat the driver with courtesy.
6. No leaning out of the windows.
7. No swearing or vulgarity.
8. No fighting.

TALKING IT OVER. Work with a partner. Decide which rules you think are more important and which are less important. Put the rules in order from most important to least important. Share your list with your classmates.

WRITING AND SHARING. Does your school have bus rules? If so, write down each rule. Talk with your classmates. Compare your school's rules to Kennedy's rules.

UNIT 9
ARMS STRAIGHT OUT!

🔊 **TUNING IN.** Look at the pictures. Listen to Mr. Fields. Do what he tells you.

Stand up straight!
Feet apart!
Raise your arms!
Point your arms straight out.
Touch your right hand to your left foot. Don't bend your knees!
Now straighten up!
Touch your left hand to your right foot.
And straighten up again.

READING ALONG. Juan and his classmates do exercises every day in PE.

First they warm up. They do 50 jumping jacks.

Next they stretch. They touch their toes 40 times.

Then they do 20 push-ups.

They also do 50 leg stretches.

Then they run in place for 15 minutes.

Last they cool down. They walk in place for 5 minutes.

FINDING OUT.

How fit are you? Make a chart like this one.

▲ How many jumping jacks can you do?
▲ How many push-ups can you do?
▲ How many pull-ups can you do?
▲ How many times can you touch your toes?
▲ How many times can you skip rope?

TUNING IN.

How fit are Chip and his friends? Point to the clock that matches what each student says.

1.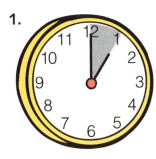
2.
3.
4.
5.
6.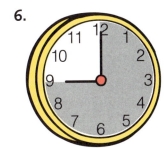
7.

JUST FOR Fun

Design a daily exercise program. What exercises will you do at least three times a week? For how many minutes will you do each exercise? Make a chart like this one.

Exercise	Mon.	Tues.	Wed.	Thurs.	Fri.	Sat.	Sun.
Jumping jacks	5 minutes		5 minutes		5 minutes		

Unit 9   67

READING ALOUD. Name each activity.

These are all good fitness activities.

fast dancing

jogging

speed walking

jumping rope

gymnastics

track and field

weight training

tinikling

WRITING AND SHARING.

Which fitness activities do you enjoy most? Which do you enjoy least? Make a list.

▲ Number a sheet of paper from 1 to 8.

▲ Write the name of the activity you like *most* next to number 1.

▲ Write the name of the activity you like *least* next to number 8.

▲ Add the names of other activities in the order of how much you like them.

Share your list with a partner.

 **JUST FOR Fun**

Teach your classmates a game or a dance, such as the tinikling, that may be new to them. Show them *how* to play the game or *do* the dance.

ACTING IT OUT. Try this conversation with your classmates.

Chip: My favorite team sport is soccer.
Lori: Mine, too! I love soccer!
Juan: I like baseball more.
Shelley: My favorite individual sport is swimming.
Juan: Mine, too. I love swimming!
Chip: Not me. I like riding my bike.
Lori: My favorite two-person sport is table tennis.
Shelley: I like badminton.

TUNING IN. Listen as Mr. Fields names some sports. Hold up one finger when you hear the name of an individual sport. Hold up two fingers when you hear the name of a two-person sport. Hold up three fingers when you hear the name of a team sport.

TALKING IT OVER. Work in small groups. Find out each person's favorite and least favorite sports. Does everyone in your group agree? Make a chart like this one.

	Favorite sports	Least favorite sports
Individual sports		
Two-person sports		
Team sports		

ACTING IT OUT. Try these conversations with a partner.

TUNING IN. Look at the tape measure and the ruler. There are three feet in a yard. Listen as each student tells you how far he or she can throw a baseball. Then write the answer to each question.

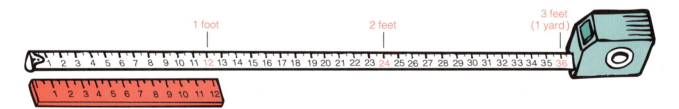

FINDING OUT.

How many steps does it take you to walk 100 yards? Make a guess. Then check your guess by counting your steps as you walk 100 yards.

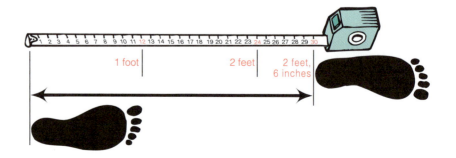

70 Unit 9

GUESSING AND CHECKING. Work in small groups. Make a chart like this one. For each sport in the chart put your guess in each column. Then check your guesses.

Name	Wiffle Ball Throw		Standing Jump		Running Jump	
	Guess	Actual	Guess	Actual	Guess	Actual
1.						
2.						
3.						
4.						
5.						
6.						

↑ Put your names in this column.

↑ How far can you throw a wiffle ball? Put your guess in this column.

↑ How far did you throw the ball? Put your actual distance in this column.

↑ How long a standing jump can you do? Put your guess in this column.

↑ Put your actual distance in this column.

↑ How far can you jump? Put your guess in this column.

↑ How far did you jump? Put your actual distance in this column.

GRAPHING IT.

How far can each person in your group throw a wiffle ball? Make a bar graph like this one.

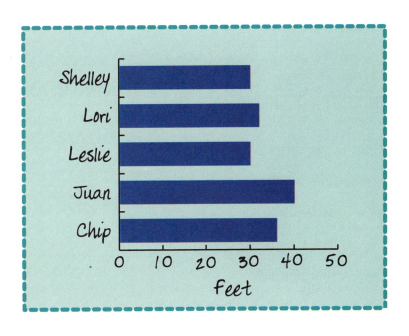

Unit 9 71

LISTENING IN. What are the students going to do now?

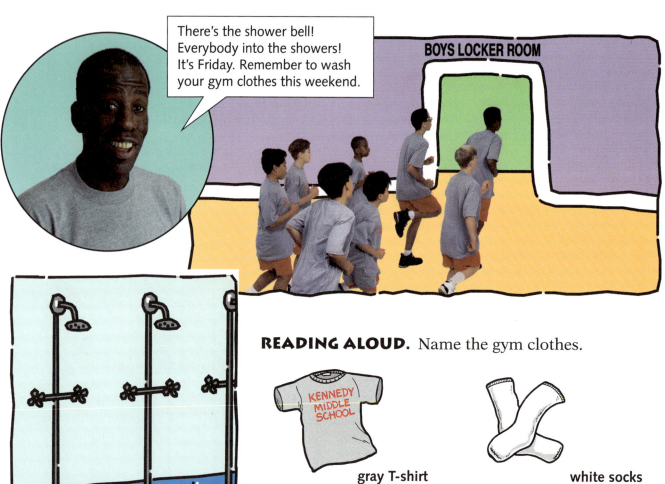

"There's the shower bell! Everybody into the showers! It's Friday. Remember to wash your gym clothes this weekend."

READING ALOUD. Name the gym clothes.

gray T-shirt

white socks

black or white sneakers

red gym shorts

I hate suiting up!

THINKING ABOUT IT.

Work with a partner. Discuss the pros and cons of having to suit up for PE. Make a chart like this one.

PROS	CONS

UNIT 10
MY FAVORITE CLASS IS ART!

Mr. Glaze: Look at this painting. Who's the artist?
Juan: Van Gogh.
Mr. Glaze: Good! What's the name of the painting?
Lori: *Starry Night*.
Mr. Glaze: That's right! You can see *Starry Night* at the Museum of Modern Art in New York City.

ACTING IT OUT. Try this conversation with your classmates.

Mr. Glaze: Do you like *Starry Night*?
Juan: Yes!
Neelam: I love it!
Mr. Glaze: Why? What do you like about the painting?
Neelam: The colors. I like the colors!
Juan: Me, too!

READING ALOUD.

Name the colors on van Gogh's palette.

TALKING IT OVER. Look at *Starry Night* again. What colors did van Gogh use? What's your favorite color?

WRITING AND SHARING. Make a list of things that are your favorite color. Share your list with a partner.

74 Unit 10

LISTENING IN. What is the class talking about?

Mr. Glaze: Tell me more about the colors.
Juan: I see a lot of different kinds of blue in the painting.
Lori: And there are a lot of different kinds of yellow, too.

READING ALONG. Read about some color families.

These colors belong to the blue family.

- This is light blue.
- This is dark blue.
- Blue is a cool color.

These colors belong to the yellow family.

- This is light yellow.
- This is bright yellow.
- Yellow is a warm color.

FIGURING IT OUT.

Look at van Gogh's palette again. Which are the cool colors? Which are the warm colors? Make a chart like this one.

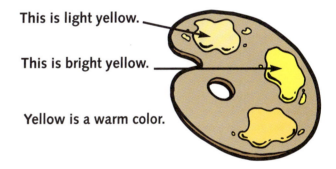

TUNING IN. You can find colors all around you! Listen to Mr. Glaze. Follow his directions.

Unit 10   75

LISTENING IN. What is the class looking at?

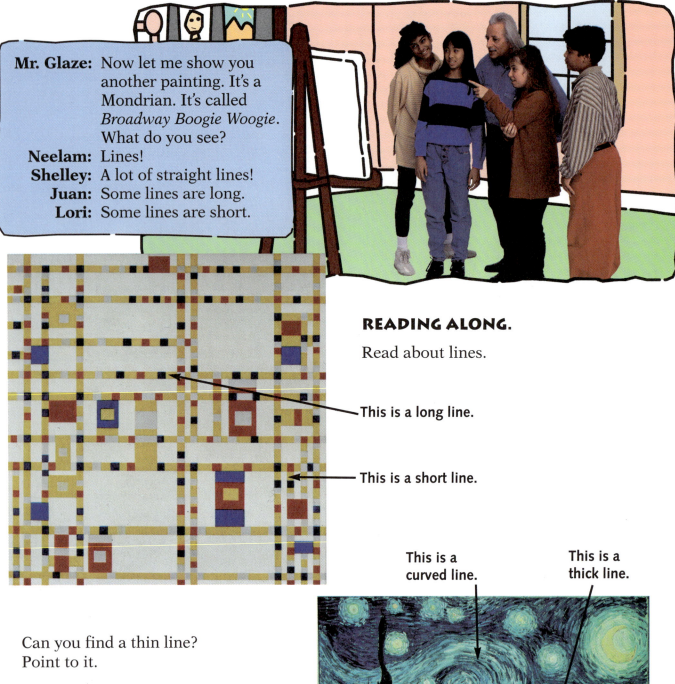

Mr. Glaze: Now let me show you another painting. It's a Mondrian. It's called *Broadway Boogie Woogie*. What do you see?
Neelam: Lines!
Shelley: A lot of straight lines!
Juan: Some lines are long.
Lori: Some lines are short.

READING ALONG.

Read about lines.

This is a long line.

This is a short line.

This is a curved line.

This is a thick line.

Can you find a thin line? Point to it.

Point to other curved lines in van Gogh's painting.

THINKING ABOUT IT.

How do these two paintings differ from each other? Talk with your classmates.

LISTENING IN. What do the students see in the painting?

Mr. Glaze: What else do you see in the painting by Mondrian?
Neelam: Lots of squares!
Lori: Red and yellow squares.
Juan: And blue squares.
Lori: I see rectangles, too.

THINKING ABOUT IT. Lines make shapes. How many shapes can you name? Which shapes are made of straight lines? Which shapes are made of curved lines?

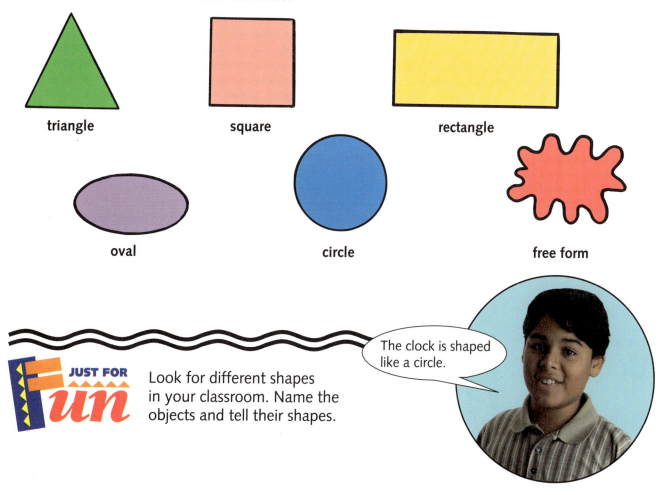

triangle

square

rectangle

oval

circle

free form

JUST FOR Fun Look for different shapes in your classroom. Name the objects and tell their shapes.

The clock is shaped like a circle.

Unit 10   77

LISTENING IN. What are the students looking at?

Mr. Glaze: This is what one of my students in second period created. It's called a *collage*. What do you see in the collage?
Neelam: I see letters.
Juan: I see words.

READING ALONG.
Read about the collage.

Some letters have curved lines.

Some letters have straight lines.

Some letters have both straight and curved lines.

FIGURING IT OUT.

Name the letters that have straight lines. Name the letters that have curved lines. Can you find any shapes in the letters? What are they?

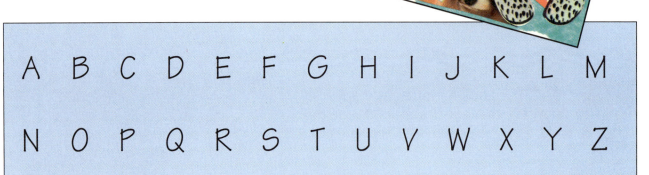

FINDING OUT. Gather the materials you need to make a collage.

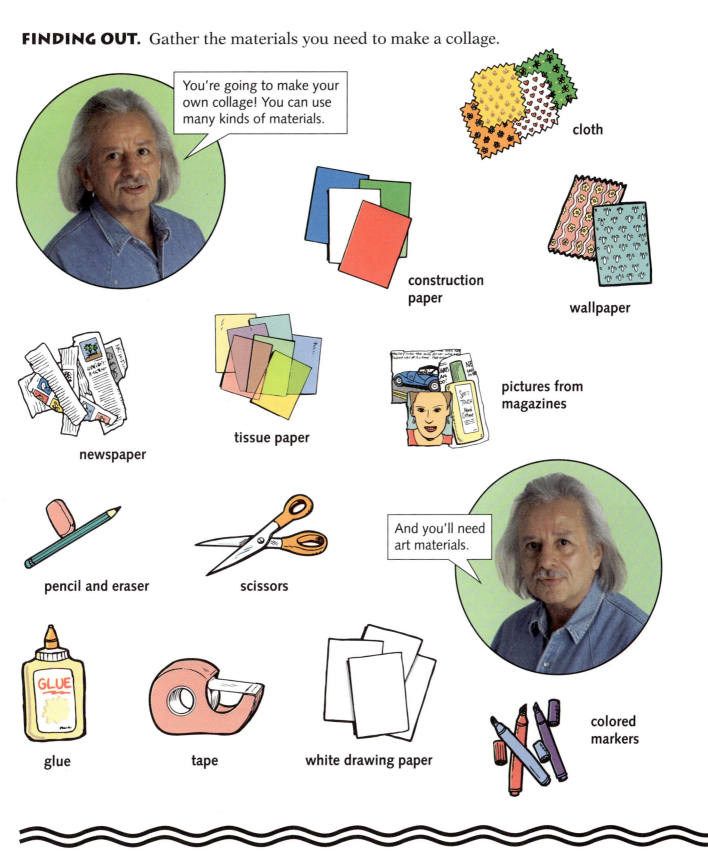

"You're going to make your own collage! You can use many kinds of materials."

cloth

construction paper

wallpaper

newspaper

tissue paper

pictures from magazines

pencil and eraser

scissors

"And you'll need art materials."

glue

tape

white drawing paper

colored markers

Work in groups of three or four. Make a collage. Use materials you might find at home—pictures, scraps of cloth, pieces of colorful paper, and so on.

Unit 10 79

FOLLOWING ALONG. Make another collage! Follow the directions.

Here's an abstract collage made from different shapes and lines. Now you make one. Do what I say.

1. Cut out four or five red triangles.

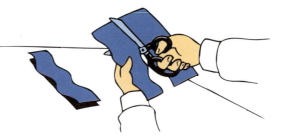

2. Cut out several blue curvy lines.

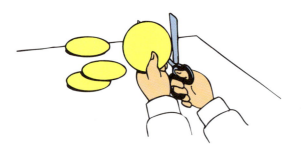

3. Cut out three or four yellow circles.

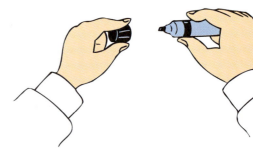

4. You'll need a black marker.

TUNING IN. Make the collage. Listen to Mr. Glaze. Follow his directions.

ON YOUR OWN. Look at *Broadway Boogie Woogie* again. Make a collage that imitates this famous painting.

80   Unit 10

UNIT 11
LET'S BE CREATIVE!

Mr. Glaze: I have another painting to show you. This one is by Chip Kowalski. It's a copy of *Starry Night*. He's in second-period art.

Each of you is going to make a copy of *Starry Night*, just like Chip did. You can use paint or colored markers.

TUNING IN. Listen to some of the students in art class. Do they like Chip's painting? Point your thumb up if a student likes the painting. Point your thumb down if he or she does not like the painting.

FOLLOWING ALONG.

Practice making lines and dots with a paintbrush. Follow the directions.

Practice making straight lines.

Let's begin by practicing how to use a paintbrush.

Now practice making curvy lines.

Practice making wavy lines.

Practice making zigzag lines.

Practice making tiny dots.

Practice making big dots.

TUNING IN. Listen to Mr. Glaze. Draw what he tells you to in the air!

FIGURING IT OUT.

Look at Chip's painting again.

▲ Find a thin line.
▲ Find a thick line.
▲ Find a short, curved line.
▲ Find a wavy line.
▲ Find a straight line.
▲ Find some tiny dots.

Here's a curved line.

TALKING IT OUT. Bring to class a picture of a painting that you like. Ask and answer with your classmates.

▲ What is the name of the painting?
▲ What lines and shapes do you see in the painting?
▲ What colors did the artist use?
▲ Who is the artist?

82   Unit 11

FIGURING IT OUT.

Look at the colors and answer the questions.

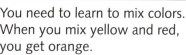

You need to learn to mix colors. When you mix yellow and red, you get orange.

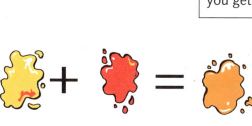

1. What color do you get when you mix yellow and red?

2. What color do you get when you mix red and blue?

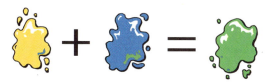

3. What color do you get when you mix yellow and blue?

4. What color do you get when you mix red and white?

5. What color do you get when you mix blue and a little black?

6. What color do you get when you mix white and black?

THINKING ABOUT IT.

What colors can you get by mixing the colors on this palette?

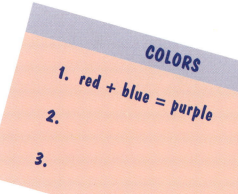

COLORS
1. red + blue = purple
2.
3.

 Paint manufacturers often give colors special names, like "arctic white" and "grass green." Give each color on this palette a special name.

Unit 11   83

LISTENING IN.

What kind of lines does Chip repeat in his painting?

Look at Chip's painting again. See how he repeats the curvy lines over and over. He uses the lines to form a pattern.

FIGURING IT OUT.

Look again at van Gogh's painting *Starry Night*. Find the patterns.

▲ What kinds of *lines* appear over and over?

▲ What kinds of *shapes* appear over and over?

▲ What *colors* appear over and over?

▲ What *objects* or *things* appear over and over?

TUNING IN. Listen as Juan and his classmates play a guessing game. Juan picked one of these pictures of living things, and his classmates are trying to guess which one. Can you figure it out?

1.
2.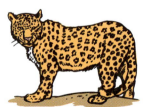
3.
4.
5.
6.

84   Unit 11

WRITING AND SHARING.

What patterns do you see in your classroom? Work in pairs. Make a list. Share the list with other pairs in your class.

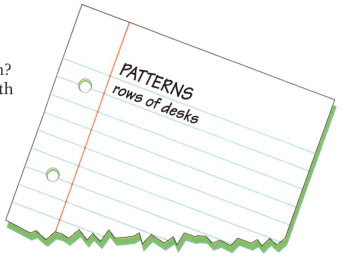

TALKING IT OVER.

Look at these pieces of artwork from different parts of the world. What patterns do you find in each one?

Navajo carpet

Canadian Indian basket

African carved mask

Aboriginal bark painting

 Bring something from home that represents your native culture. It might be artwork, something decorative, or something to wear. Share it with your classmates.

Unit 11 85

LISTENING IN.

What material does Lori want to use in her painting?

Lori: Mr. Glaze, can I use yarn in my painting?
Mr. Glaze: That's a clever idea! The yarn will change the *texture* of your painting. The texture of a painting can be rough or smooth.

WRITING AND SHARING.

Look around your classroom. Which objects have a rough texture? Which objects have a smooth texture? Work with a partner. Make a chart like the one below. Share your chart with your classmates.

Things that are smooth	Things that are rough

FOLLOWING ALONG. Make a frame for your painting or collage. Follow the directions.

1. First glue your painting to a piece of poster board that is larger than the painting. Choose a contrasting color.

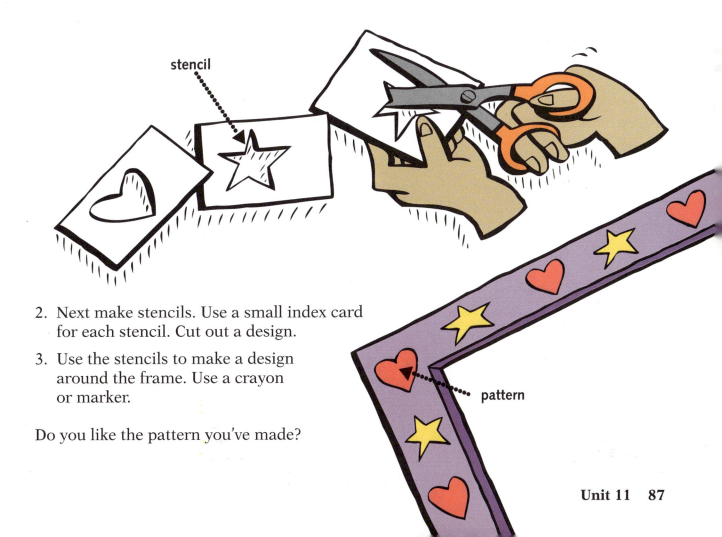

2. Next make stencils. Use a small index card for each stencil. Cut out a design.

3. Use the stencils to make a design around the frame. Use a crayon or marker.

Do you like the pattern you've made?

TUNING IN. Chip and Juan are looking at the paintings at the Kennedy art show. Listen to their comments. Which painting is Chip describing?

Welcome to our art show!

A.

B.

TALKING IT OUT. How are Lori's and Shelley's paintings different from each other? How are they the same?

UNIT 12 WHERE IN THE WORLD IS...?

TUNING IN. Look at the overhead projector. Listen as the students make guesses. For each guess, point your thumb up if you think it is a good guess. Point your thumb down if you think it is a bad guess.

LISTENING IN. What did Ms. Goldstein show the students on the overhead projector?

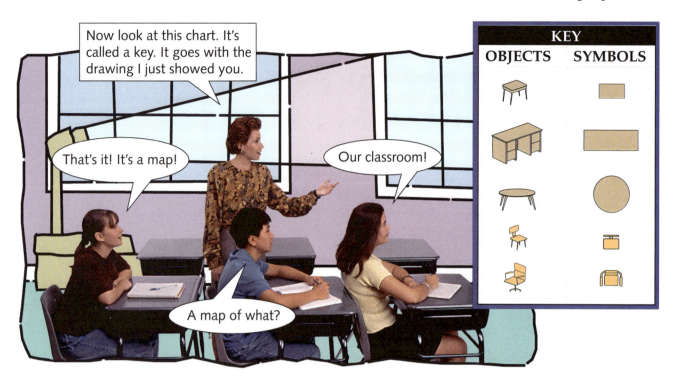

MAPPING IT OUT.

Draw a map of your classroom. First make a key. Then, using your key, make the map.

90   Unit 12

LISTENING IN.

What are the students going to make?

Here's a map of our school. Make a new school map, using symbols. You'll need to make a key.

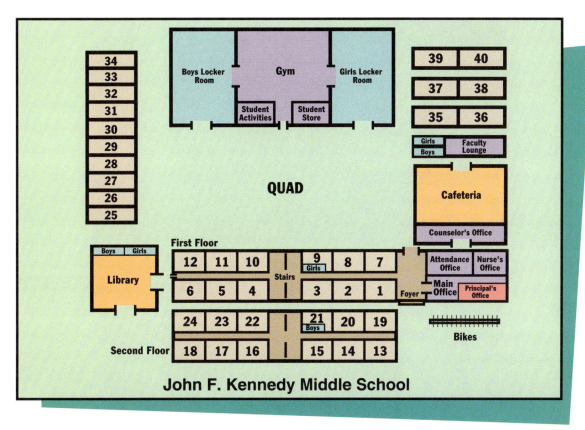

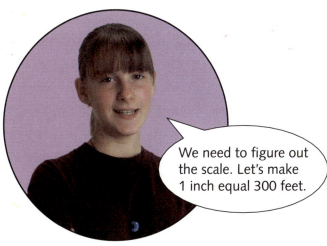

We need to figure out the scale. Let's make 1 inch equal 300 feet.

MAPPING IT OUT.

Divide the campus into four parts. Divide the class into four groups. Each group should be responsible for drawing a map of one of the parts, or quadrants. Make the map as close to scale as you can. Then put your maps together to make one large map.

Unit 12   91

ACTING IT OUT.

Try this conversation with your classmates.

Ms. Goldstein: This is a map of our neighborhood. Where is our school?
Juan: It's on Coolidge Avenue.
Ms. Goldstein: Be more specific.
Neelam: It's between MacArthur Boulevard and 23rd Street.
Ms. Goldstein: What else does the map tell you?
Maria: Well, our school is north of the Freeway.
Ms. Goldstein: And what else?
Juan: It's south of Lincoln Avenue.

TUNING IN.

After school Ms. Goldstein has an appointment not far from Kennedy Middle School. She decides to walk. Listen as Ms. Goldstein plans her route. Trace the route on the map. Where is she going?

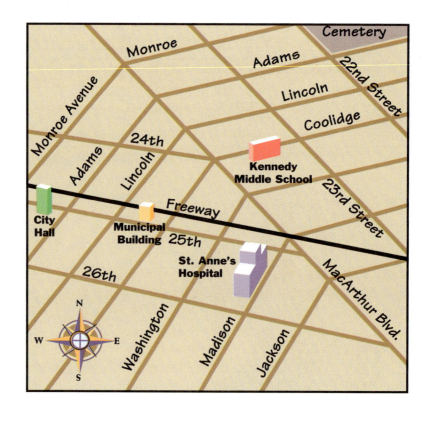

LISTENING IN. What are the students looking at?

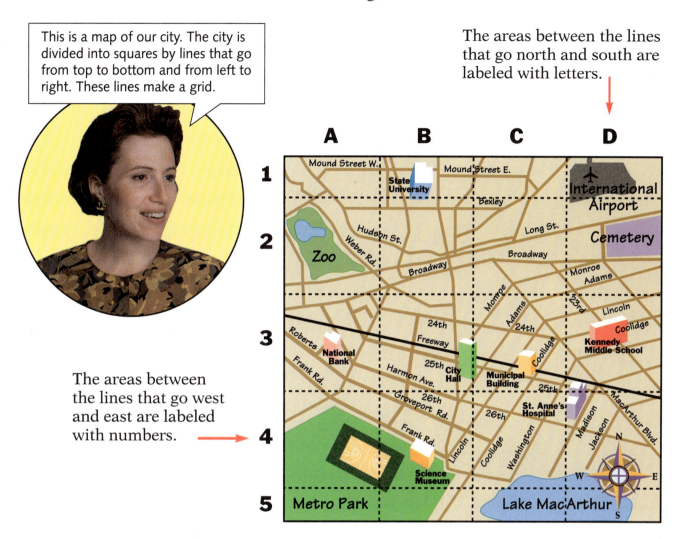

This is a map of our city. The city is divided into squares by lines that go from top to bottom and from left to right. These lines make a grid.

The areas between the lines that go north and south are labeled with letters.

The areas between the lines that go west and east are labeled with numbers.

USING A GRID. Find places on the map.

1. Name something that is located in square A2.
2. Name something that is located in square D1.
3. Name something that is located in square B4.
4. Name something that is located in square B1.
5. Name something that is located in square A3.
6. Where is City Hall located?
7. Where is Kennedy Middle School located?
8. Where is the Cemetery located?
9. Where is Lake MacArthur located?
10. Where is St. Anne's Hospital located?

MAPPING IT OUT. Work with a partner. Make a map of your school's neighborhood. Make the map as close to scale as you can. Include grid lines and labels. Share your map with your classmates.

Unit 12   93

READING ALOUD.

Read the name of each state. Read the name of each city shown on this map.

This is a map of the United States. Trace the border of the United States with your finger.

TUNING IN. Look at the map. Listen to Ms. Goldstein. As she names each state, point to it on the map. Now listen to Ms. Goldstein as she names each city. Point to it on the map.

FIGURING IT OUT. Name places on the map.

1. Name a large state.
2. Name a tiny state.
3. Name a state that is east of California.
4. Name a state that is north of Texas.
5. Name a state that is south of New York.
6. Name a state that touches one of the Great Lakes.
7. Name a state that borders the Pacific Ocean.
8. Name a state that borders Mexico.
9. Name a state that borders Canada.
10. Name a state that is located on the Atlantic Ocean.

READING ALOUD. Name the important land regions shown on this map.

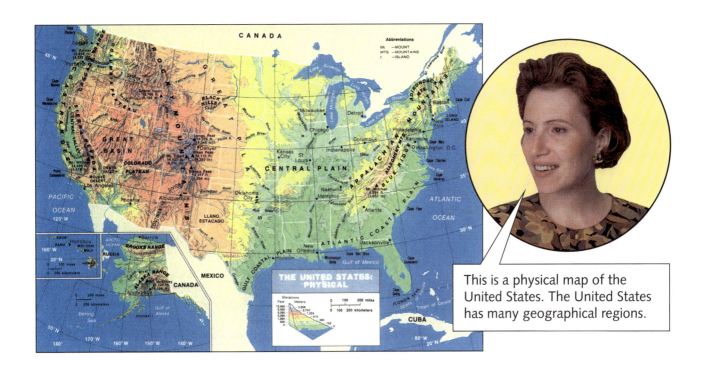

This is a physical map of the United States. The United States has many geographical regions.

This is a drawing of some of the different landforms in the United States.

READING ALOUD. Name the landforms.

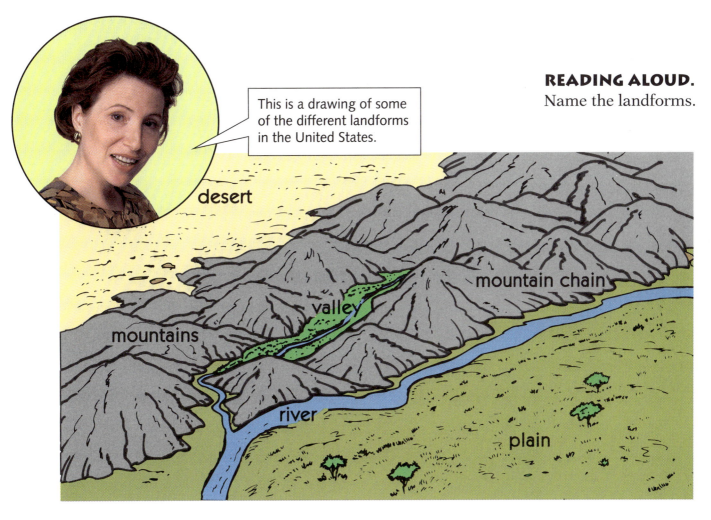

Unit 12   95

READING ALOUD.
Read the labels on the world map.

This map shows the entire world. Can you find the equator? It is an imaginary line around the middle of the Earth. The equator is a line of latitude. There are other lines of latitude north and south of the equator.

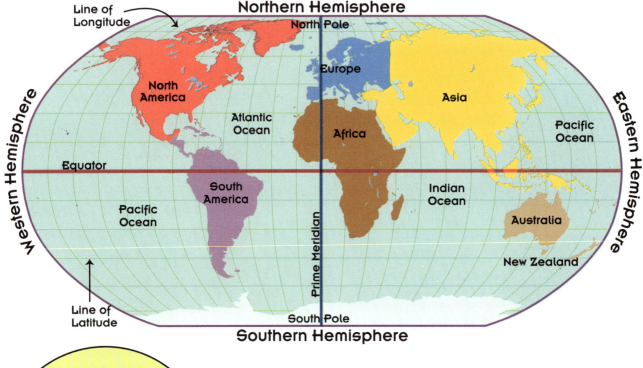

Can you find the prime meridian? The prime meridian is a line of longitude. There are other lines of longitude east and west of the prime meridian.

TUNING IN.

Look at the map of the world. Listen to Ms. Goldstein. Follow her directions.

FINDING OUT. Use a globe or an atlas to answer these questions.

1. Is China north of the equator or south of the equator?

2. Is Argentina north of the equator or south of the equator?

3. Is the United States to the west of the prime meridian or to the east?

4. Is the United States in the western or in the eastern hemisphere?

96   Unit 12

UNIT 13

LET'S FIND OUT!

Ms. Yoshida-Johnson: I'm going to show you a powder. What do you think it is? Guess.
Juan: Sugar?
Neelam: Salt?
Ms. Yoshida-Johnson: It looks like both salt and sugar, but it's neither. We're going to do an experiment. We're going to discover more about some mystery powders. Here are the materials we'll need for our experiment.

3 squares of black construction paper for each student

paper cups

paper towels

3 plastic spoons for each student

hand lenses

🔊 **TUNING IN.** Look at the picture. Listen as Ms. Yoshida-Johnson names the materials for the experiment. Point to each object or the objects as she names them.

Unit 13   97

"A good way to learn more about our mystery powders is to find out how each one tastes, looks, feels, and smells. Show me the part of the body that you use to taste with."

READING ALOUD.

Read about the *senses*.

You taste with your tongue.

You see with your eyes.

"Each of you should have a paper towel. I'll put a little of each powder on your paper towel."

You feel with your fingertips.

You smell with your nose.

Let's taste each powder. Each one is safe to taste. First wash your hands. Then lick your finger. Put it in the powder on your paper towel. Taste the powder. We'll keep track of what we discover on a mystery powders chart.

TALKING IT OVER.

Ask and answer with your classmates.

▲ How does corn starch taste?
▲ How does baking soda taste?
▲ How does sugar taste?

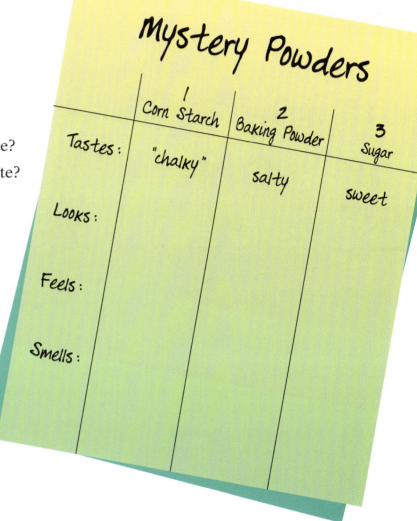

🎧 **TUNING IN.** Here is a list of common foods. Listen to the directions and tell whether each food tastes *salty* or *sweet*.

bananas	peanuts	ice cream
potato chips	pancake syrup	french fries
jam	bacon	pretzels
cookies	pizza	watermelon

Unit 13   99

FINDING OUT. Look carefully at each powder.

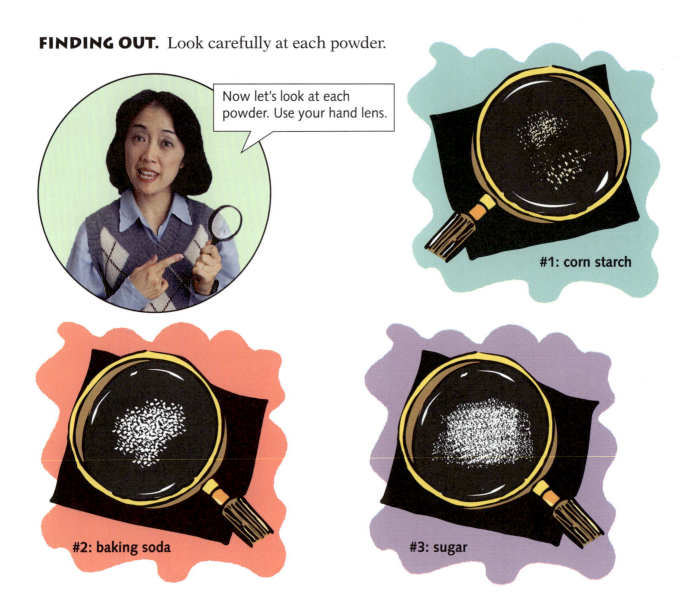

"Now let's look at each powder. Use your hand lens."

#1: corn starch

#2: baking soda

#3: sugar

TALKING IT OVER. Ask and answer with your classmates.

▲ Do the powders look the same?

▲ Which powder has large grains?
Which powder has very tiny grains?
Which powder is the most "powdery"?

▲ Which powder is the whitest?
Which powder is the least white?

▲ Can you name something else you would find in the kitchen that is grainy? What is it?

▲ Can you name something else you would find in the kitchen that is very powdery? What is it?

FIGURING IT OUT. Follow these directions.

1. Rub each powder into a piece of the black paper.

2. Then blow the loose powder away.

3. Which paper has the most powder left on it? Why?

ACTING IT OUT.

Try this conversation with your classmates.

Ms. Yoshida-Johnson:	Put down your hand lenses. Let's feel the powders. Do they feel the same?
Juan:	No. Powder number 3 feels grainy.
Neelam:	Powder number 2 feels smooth.
Tran:	Powder number 1 feels like silk. It feels silky.
Ms. Yoshida-Johnson:	Now smell each powder. Do any of the powders have a smell?

READING ALOUD.

Read the complete chart.

TUNING IN. Listen to the short conversations. Each conversation describes things you taste, see, feel, or smell. As you listen, show what each conversation is about by pointing to your mouth, eyes, fingertips, or nose.

Mystery Powders

	1 Corn Starch	2 Baking Soda	3 Sugar
Tastes:	"chalky"	salty	sweet
Looks:	powdery	tiny grains	grainy
Feels:	smooth	sort of grainy	grainy
Smells:	none	none	none

Work with a partner. Make a list of foods and spices you might find in the kitchen. Try to describe how each food or spice tastes and smells. Share your lists with classmates.

Unit 13   101

FINDING OUT. Look carefully at each powder and complete the charts.

Now we'll add vinegar to each powder. What do you think will happen?

Corn starch gets thick and then turns hard.

Baking soda fizzes and bubbles.

Sugar dissolves.

Never mix household cleaning products! It could be very dangerous!

VINEGAR TEST

POWDER	WHAT HAPPENS
Corn Starch	Gets thick, hardens
Baking Soda	
Sugar	

102   Unit 13

"Now let's add iodine. Who knows what iodine is used for?"

Corn starch turns red, then deep purple or black.

Baking soda turns yellowish-orange.

Sugar turns yellow—the color of iodine.

IODINE TEST

POWDER	WHAT HAPPENS
Corn Starch	Turns red, then black
Baking Soda	
Sugar	

TUNING IN.

Listen as Ms. Yoshida-Johnson describes some powders. For each statement, point your thumb up if it is true. Point your thumb down if it is false.

THINKING ABOUT IT. Ask and answer with your classmates.

▲ What do you think will happen if you add more iodine to each powder? Will the color change or stay the same?

▲ What do you think will happen if you mix corn starch and sugar and then add iodine? Will the mixture still turn purple or black?

FINDING OUT.

Find out how foods change when you put iodine on them. Make a chart like the one below.

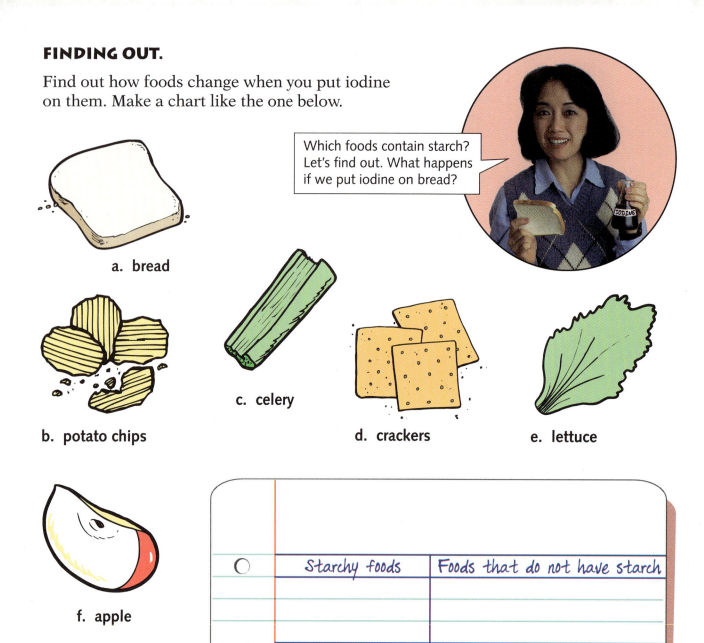

a. bread
b. potato chips
c. celery
d. crackers
e. lettuce
f. apple

TALKING IT OUT. Ask and answer with your classmates.

▲ What happens to bread when you put iodine on it?
▲ What happens to celery when you put iodine on it?
▲ What happens to a cracker when you put iodine on it?
▲ Which foods have starch in them? How can you tell?
▲ Which foods do not have starch in them? How can you tell?

ON YOUR OWN. Make a chart called "The Tools of a Scientist." Draw pictures of some of the important tools scientists use — the microscope, for example. Learn the names of these tools.

UNIT 14 LET'S CELEBRATE!

Ms. Goldstein: We don't have school next Monday. Does anyone know why?
Neelam: Is it a holiday?
Ms. Goldstein: Yes, it is! It's Presidents' Day. It's a national holiday.
Juan: What's a national holiday?
Ms. Goldstein: Well, it's when we celebrate important events or honor special people.
Tran: What are the other national holidays?
Maria: How many do we have? When are they?
Ms. Goldstein: Suppose we find out! Let's find out more about important days in our history. Work in small groups. Each group will study one of our national holidays.

TUNING IN. "America, the Beautiful" is one of our country's most beloved songs. Listen to the song.

Unit 14   105

FIGURING IT OUT.

Look at the calendar. Make a chart that shows each national holiday and when it is.

Good! Everyone is in a group. Let's make a chart that shows the national holidays and when they are. Look at the calendar.

National Holiday	Date
Martin Luther King, Jr. Day	Third Monday in January

Presidents' Day is in February. This year it's on February 21.

TALKING IT OVER.

Look at the chart and the calendar. Tell when each holiday takes place.

FINDING OUT.

Make an international calendar that shows important holidays from around the world.

Martin Luther King, Jr.'s birthday is in January. This year it's on . . .

TUNING IN. Look at the calendar. Answer Ms. Goldstein's questions.

JANUARY

SUN	MON	TUE	WED	THU	FRI	SAT
••	••	••	••	••	••	1
2	3	4	5	6	7	8
9	10	11	12	13	14	15
16	17	18	19	20	21	22
23/30	24/31	25	26	27	28	29

FEBRUARY

SUN	MON	TUE	WED	THU	FRI	SAT
••	••	1	2	3	4	5
6	7	8	9	10	11	12
13	14	15	16	17	18	19
20	21	22	23	24	25	26
27	28	••	••	••	••	••

MARCH

SUN	MON	TUE	WED	THU	FRI	SAT
••	••	1	2	3	4	5
6	7	8	9	10	11	12
13	14	15	16	17	18	19
20	21	22	23	24	25	26
27	28	29	30	31	••	••

APRIL

SUN	MON	TUE	WED	THU	FRI	SAT
••	••	••	••	••	1	2
3	4	5	6	7	8	9
10	11	12	13	14	15	16
17	18	19	20	21	22	23
24	25	26	27	28	29	30

MAY

SUN	MON	TUE	WED	THU	FRI	SAT
1	2	3	4	5	6	7
8	9	10	11	12	13	14
15	16	17	18	19	20	21
22	23	24	25	26	27	28
29	30	31	••	••	••	••

JUNE

SUN	MON	TUE	WED	THU	FRI	SAT
••	••	••	1	2	3	4
5	6	7	8	9	10	11
12	13	14	15	16	17	18
19	20	21	22	23	24	25
26	27	28	29	30	••	••

JULY

SUN	MON	TUE	WED	THU	FRI	SAT
••	••	••	••	••	1	2
3	4	5	6	7	8	9
10	11	12	13	14	15	16
17	18	19	20	21	22	23
24/31	25	26	27	28	29	30

AUGUST

SUN	MON	TUE	WED	THU	FRI	SAT
••	1	2	3	4	5	6
7	8	9	10	11	12	13
14	15	16	17	18	19	20
21	22	23	24	25	26	27
28	29	30	31	••	••	••

SEPTEMBER

SUN	MON	TUE	WED	THU	FRI	SAT
••	••	••	••	1	2	3
4	5	6	7	8	9	10
11	12	13	14	15	16	17
18	19	20	21	22	23	24
25	26	27	28	29	30	••

OCTOBER

SUN	MON	TUE	WED	THU	FRI	SAT
••	••	••	••	••	••	1
2	3	4	5	6	7	8
9	10	11	12	13	14	15
16	17	18	19	20	21	22
23/30	24/31	25	26	27	28	29

NOVEMBER

SUN	MON	TUE	WED	THU	FRI	SAT
••	••	1	2	3	4	5
6	7	8	9	10	11	12
13	14	15	16	17	18	19
20	21	22	23	24	25	26
27	28	29	30	••	••	••

DECEMBER

SUN	MON	TUE	WED	THU	FRI	SAT
••	••	••	••	1	2	3
4	5	6	7	8	9	10
11	12	13	14	15	16	17
18	19	20	21	22	23	24
25	26	27	28	29	30	31

JUST FOR Fun

Choose a holiday that is important to you and your family. Draw a picture of your family celebrating the holiday. Share your drawing with your classmates.

ACTING IT OUT.

Practice the students' Columbus Day play with your classmates.

Columbus: I will sail west to Asia. The Indies have gold and silver and spices!
King Ferdinand: We will pay for the voyage, and we will give you three ships and a crew of sailors.
Queen Isabella: Spain will be rich! You will be called Admiral of the Ocean Sea!
Columbus: Thank you, Queen Isabella. Thank you, King Ferdinand.

FIGURING IT OUT. Look at the map. Answer the questions.

1. What ocean did Columbus sail across?
2. On what date did Columbus reach land?
3. What is the name of the island that he landed on?
4. On what date did he sail for home?
5. How many months did Columbus's voyage take?

READING ALONG.

Read about the first Thanksgiving.

Our group studied Thanksgiving. We drew a picture of the first Thanksgiving, and we made a timeline that shows what the first year was like for the Pilgrims who landed at Plymouth.

The Pilgrims celebrate Thanksgiving.

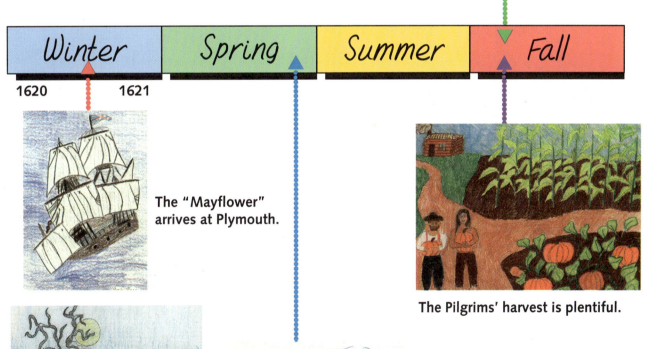

1620   1621

The "Mayflower" arrives at Plymouth.

The Pilgrims' harvest is plentiful.

Harsh winter. Many pilgrims get sick and die.

The Wampanoag Indians help the Pilgrims. They teach them how to grow corn and pumpkins. The Wampanoag also teach the Pilgrims how to hunt and fish.

Unit 14   109

"Our group made a bulletin board to celebrate Presidents' Day."

1.

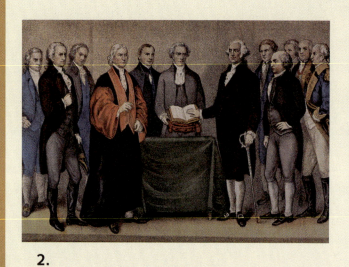

2.

3.

FIGURING IT OUT. Learn more about the lives of George Washington and Abraham Lincoln. Then match each caption with the correct picture.

a. Revolutionary War general.

b. Known for his honesty.

c. Our first president.

d. Shot in 1865.

e. President during the Civil War.

f. Said "Slavery is . . . evil."

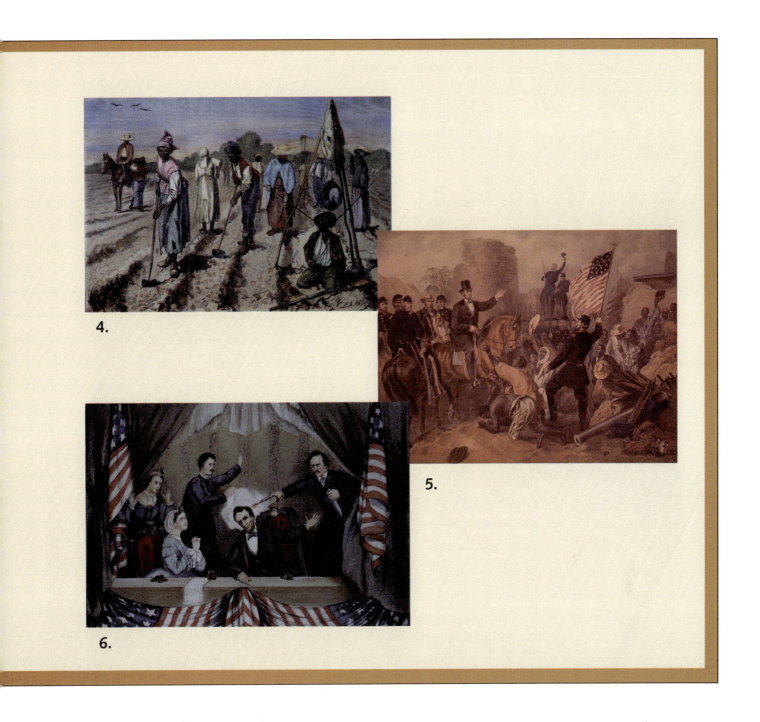

4.

5.

6.

You can find pictures of important Americans on our coins. Draw three coins. Find out who is pictured on each coin. Then write his name under the picture of that coin.

"The U.S. flag and bald eagle are national symbols. Many people display the flag on the Fourth of July, Independence Day."

READING ALONG.

Read about the American flag.

Each star stands for one of the fifty states.

Each stripe stands for one of the thirteen original colonies.

TUNING IN.

Listen to The Pledge of Allegiance. Then recite it with your classmates.

I pledge allegiance to the flag of the United States of America, and to the republic for which it stands, one nation, under God, indivisible, with liberty and justice for all.

WRITING AND SHARING.

Write a short description of the bald eagle. Share it with your classmates.

free

strong

proud

THE THIRTEEN ORIGINAL COLONIES

part of Massachusetts
New Hampshire
Massachusetts
New York
Rhode Island
Connecticut
Pennsylvania
New Jersey
Delaware
Maryland
Virginia
North Carolina
South Carolina
Georgia
Atlantic Ocean

UNIT 15
WHAT'S MATH GOOD FOR, ANYWAY?

Mrs. Delgado: One of my students made this last year. What do you think it is, class? Guess!
Juan: It's a box.
Maria: Maybe it's a doll house.
Neelam: Or maybe a house for an animal!
Juan: I know what it is! It's a *model*!
Mrs. Delgado: You're right! It's our . . .

LISTENING IN. What are the students going to make?

Mrs. Delgado: You're right. It's our classroom! Let's make a model of our classroom. You'll need graph paper. Use standard or metric measurement, so you'll need either a yardstick or a meterstick.
Juan: What do we do first?
Mrs. Delgado: You'll see. We'll work together.

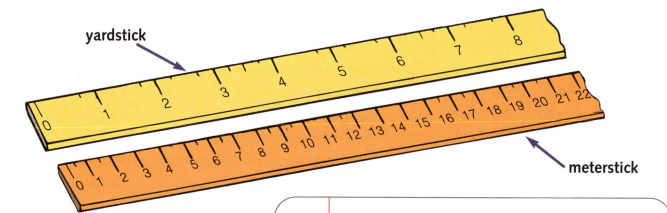

GUESSING AND CHECKING.

Find five classroom objects to measure both in inches and in centimeters. First estimate the length of each object. Then check your estimates by measuring the objects. Make a chart like this one.

Classroom object	Inches		Centimeters	
	Estimate	Actual	Estimate	Actual

 Bring in a model of something to share with your classmates.

114   Unit 15

Let's estimate the dimensions of our classroom. I'll write down each group's guesses on the board. Then we'll measure the room.

LISTENING IN.

What are the students estimating?

TUNING IN.

Listen as Mrs. Delgado asks some questions about your classroom. Write down your estimates.

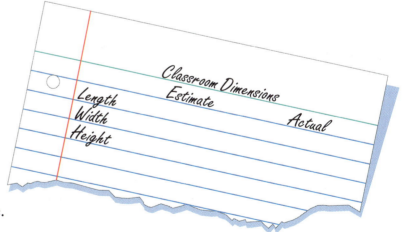

GUESSING AND CHECKING.

Estimate the dimensions of your classroom. Then check your estimates. Make a chart like this one.

TALKING IT OVER. Answer the questions with your classmates.

▲ What is the length of your classroom?

▲ What is the width of your classroom?

▲ How high is the ceiling?

▲ How wide is the doorway to your classroom? How high is it?

▲ How many windows are there? How wide are they? How high?

Unit 15   115

FINDING OUT.

First make a list of the furniture in your classroom. Then measure the dimensions of each piece of furniture. Write the dimensions on your list.

Let's measure the furniture in our room.

TUNING IN. Listen as Mrs. Delgado describes some classroom furniture. Look at the pictures and point to each item as she describes it.

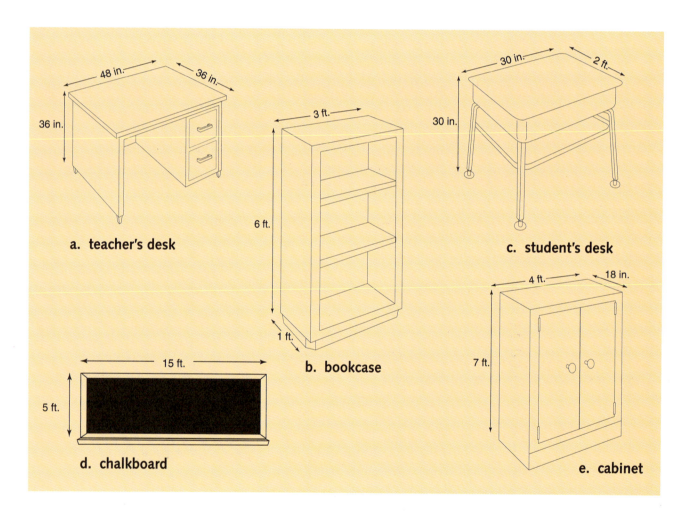

a. teacher's desk
b. bookcase
c. student's desk
d. chalkboard
e. cabinet

TALKING IT OVER. Answer the questions with your classmates.

▲ How wide is each student's desk in your classroom? How deep, including the seat?
▲ Does your room have bookcases or cabinets? How high are they? How wide?

116   Unit 15

THINKING ABOUT IT. Look at illustration A. It shows you a bird's eye view of the teacher's desk. What do you do to find the area of the top of the desk?

Now look at illustration B. What do you do to find how much space the desk takes up?

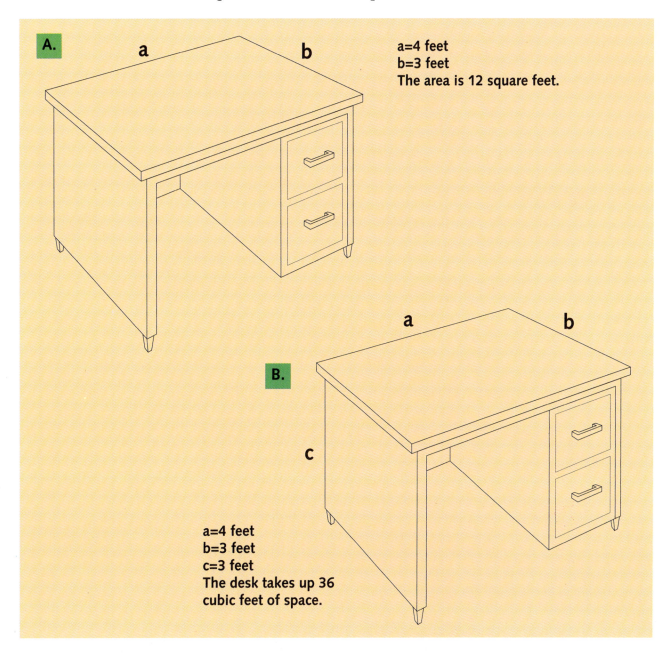

A.
a=4 feet
b=3 feet
The area is 12 square feet.

B.
a=4 feet
b=3 feet
c=3 feet
The desk takes up 36 cubic feet of space.

FIGURING IT OUT. Answer the questions.

1. How much *area* does a student's desk in your classroom take up?
2. How much *total space* does it take up?
3. How much *area* does the teacher's desk in your classroom take up?
4. How much *total space* does it take up?

FOLLOWING ALONG. Begin building your model. Follow the directions.

1. You're ready to make your model. First glue a sheet of graph paper to each of five sheets of thin cardboard.

2. Begin by laying out the floor. Each square inch should equal a square yard. Measure the length and the width.

3. Next draw the lines to show the perimeter.

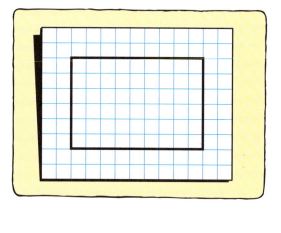

4. Then cut out the floor.

5 Now make the front and back walls the same way you made the floor.

6 Make the side walls. Don't forget the door and windows.

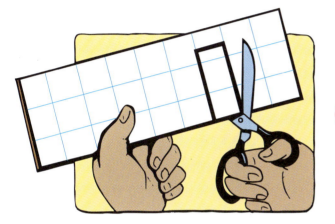

7 Now cut out the door and windows.

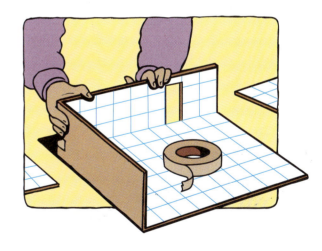

8 Finally tape the walls and floor together.

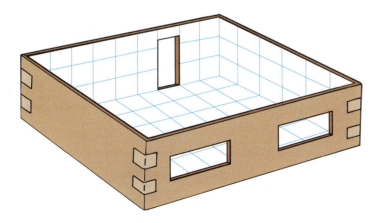

TUNING IN. Listen as Juan describes the model of his classroom. Follow along and draw what he says.

Unit 15 119

THINKING ABOUT IT.

Why do you think Juan asks this question?

This was fun, but are we ever going to use this stuff?

Many people use math in their jobs every day.

🔊 TUNING IN.

Look at the pictures and listen as each worker describes his or her job. Point to the person who is talking.

a. carpet installer

b. carpenter

c. engineer

d. roofer

e. architect

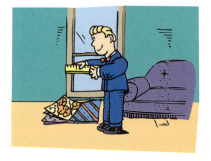

f. interior decorator

JUST FOR Fun

Add to your picture dictionary. Title the pages "People who use math in their work." Draw or clip pictures from magazines of people who use math in their work. Write the name of the occupation under each picture. Then write one thing you know about each occupation.

UNIT 16
WHAT A GREAT SCHOOL YEAR!

I know what to say when I meet people and I know people's names.
I know words like "please" and "thank you."

Ms. Reed: The school year is almost over! Let's take some time and look at the work you've done this year. Then each of you can assemble a small portfolio that shows your personal best.
Juan: Personal best?
Ms. Reed: Yes, your personal best. Do you remember the names van Gogh and Mondrian? Who were they?
Neelam: Artists!
Ms. Reed: Right! Most artists have portfolios that show their talent. They include work that they think is their very best.
Juan: But this isn't art. This is ESL.
Ms. Reed: Well, your portfolio will show your best work in English. It will show me — and others — examples of what you've learned this year.

LISTENING IN. What are the students going to tell Ms. Reed?

Let's think about what you've learned this year. Back in September, many of you didn't speak much English! How much English do you know today? Tell me. I'll write down what you say.

READING ALONG.

Read the students' list.

> I know what to say when I meet people, and I know people's names.
> I know words like "please" and "thank you."
>
> I can talk with a friend.
> I can tell about myself.
> I can describe other people.
> I can tell other people what I like and don't like.
> I can tell other people how I feel.
>
> I can answer questions (sometimes).
> I can ask questions (sometimes).
>
> I know lots of words (for things in the classroom, places at school, parts of the body, types of clothing, names of sports, things to do with friends).
>
> I can say to a friend, "Let's . . ."

WRITING AND SHARING.

Work with a partner. What other items can you add to this list? Share your list with your classmates.

JUST FOR Fun

Describe one of your classmates without telling his or her name. Can others guess who it is? Remember: Say only nice things about the person!

I'm thinking of someone who is from Mexico. She has brown hair and . . .

ACTING IT OUT. Work with a partner. Make up a short skit about two people your age. They have a problem: They don't have anything to do, and they're bored! How do they solve their problem? Act out your skit for your classmates.

"What about at school? How well can you communicate in the classroom?"

READING ALONG.

Read the students' list.

> I can understand a teacher's directions for doing an assignment. (usually)
>
> I can pay attention. (always)
>
> I can tell others when I don't understand something.
>
> I can answer a teacher's questions. (sometimes)
>
> I can follow along when the teacher explains how to make something or do something. (usually)
>
> I can understand what I'm supposed to do and what I'm not supposed to do. (almost always)
>
> I know how to get help if I have a problem. (most of the time)

WRITING AND SHARING.

Work with a partner. What other items can you add to this list? Share your list with your classmates.

ON YOUR OWN.

Think about the following questions and make a chart.

▲ When is it easy for you to understand what others are saying to you?

▲ When is it hard to understand?

▲ When is it easy for you to communicate what you want to say?

▲ When is it hard to communicate?

TALKING IT OVER. Discuss the questions with your classmates. Share your charts with each other.

TUNING IN. Listen to the students' short conversations. Answer the question that follows each one.

You didn't just learn language, did you? What else did you learn and do this year?

TUNING IN.

Listen as the students tell what they have learned or done during the year. Point to the picture that matches what each student says.

a.
b.
c.
d.
e.
f.

TALKING IT OVER. Work with a partner. Think back over the school year. Talk about the topics you studied and the things you did or made. Make a chart like this one. Share your chart with your classmates.

This year
| Topics we studied | Things we did or made |

Here's a list of some of the topics you've studied this year. You've learned a lot of important words and ideas that will help you in your other classes.

READING ALONG.

Look at Ms. Reed's list of topics. Compare your chart with this list.

Things We've Learned About or Studied This Year

- Ancient civilizations (names and dates)
- Living things (plants and animals)
- Design: color, line, shape, and pattern
- Kinds of maps
- What a scientific experiment is
- The Pilgrims
- Measurements
- The Thirteen Colonies
- Sports
- Safety in the science lab
- Landforms and bodies of water
- Chemical reactions
- How to "see" a painting with a critical eye
- Columbus's first voyage to the New World
- How to build a model to scale
- How to mix paints
- How to figure out area
- How to make a map to scale
- The lives of Washington and Lincoln
- How to use a hand lens
- Fitness and exercise

FIGURING IT OUT.

Make a mind map that shows in which class you might study each topic or do each activity on Ms. Reed's list.

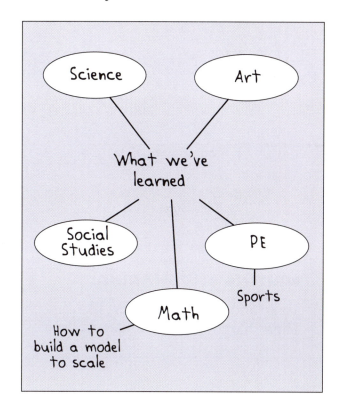

Draw a picture of yourself doing the activity you enjoyed most this year. Share your picture with your classmates.

Unit 16   125

ON YOUR OWN. Think about your ability to read and write in English. Take Ms. Reed's survey.

Reading and Writing Self-Assessment

	Always	Usually	Sometimes	Never
1. Reading is fun, and I like to find things to read that I can understand.	❏	❏	❏	❏
2. I can read schedules, signs at school, school rules, and signs in the community.	❏	❏	❏	❏
3. I can read the directions in my ESL book.	❏	❏	❏	❏
4. I can understand what I read in other classes.	❏	❏	❏	❏
5. I can fill out school forms, schedules, and charts.	❏	❏	❏	❏
6. I can make things—like maps and posters—that involve writing.	❏	❏	❏	❏
7. I can use my own drawings and words to communicate something interesting.	❏	❏	❏	❏
8. I can write simple sentences to give other people information.	❏	❏	❏	❏
9. I can do written work in my other classes.	❏	❏	❏	❏

WRITING AND SHARING.

Make and complete a chart like this one. Then share it with your classmates.

Things that are usually easy to read	Things that are usually hard to read
Things that are usually easy to write	Things that are usually hard to write

TALKING IT OVER.

Discuss the following questions with a partner.

▲ What kinds of materials are usually easy to read in English? To write in English?

▲ What kinds of materials are usually more difficult to read in English? To write in English?

THINKING ABOUT IT.

Personal best is your very best work — an assignment or something else you have done this year in this or another class.

Look again at your work. In your opinion, what is your best work? Why? Does this work show your ability to communicate in English? Does it show your ability to think? Does it show your creativity?

Tell about your personal best. Make a chart like this one.

Work I've done this year that I'm proud of	Why I'm proud of this work

LISTENING IN. What are the students going to make?

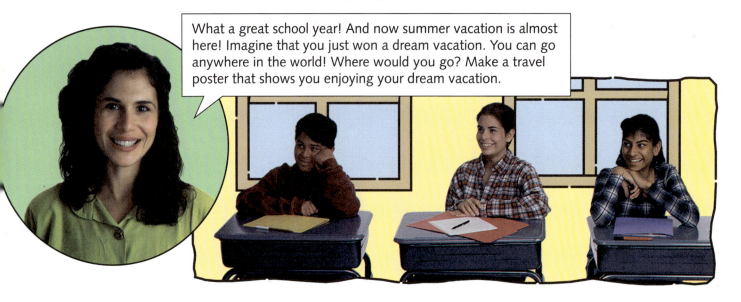

What a great school year! And now summer vacation is almost here! Imagine that you just won a dream vacation. You can go anywhere in the world! Where would you go? Make a travel poster that shows you enjoying your dream vacation.

TUNING IN. The students are sharing their posters with each other. Listen as each student describes his or her poster. Point to the picture that matches the description.

a.   b.   c.

d.   e.   f.

Where would you go on your dream vacation? Have a good time! Make a travel poster.

128   Unit 16